The Life

Worth Living

BY

JAMEKE MICHAEL BROWN

TABLE OF CONTENTS

ABOUT THE AUTHOR

Jameke's journey of faith began at the tender age of nineteen after being baptized in the Holy Spirit. After enduring successive painful tragedies in his life, he now shares his story and experience with others in the hope of illuminating the joy and peace that he has experienced through living a life in Christ, empowered by the Holy Spirit. His journey has taken him to several countries regionally and internationally preaching the gospel message of Jesus, one which he truly believes is the most important message for our world today.

His family and friends witnessed his transformation over the years and continue to verify that something extraordinary occurred to turn his life around completely from the path he was on. Over the past decade, Jameke has evolved into a music ministry and youth ministry leader as well as a commissioned lay minister in his parish and the message of the gospel has become an integral part of his life. He frequently preaches in many confirmation classes, youth groups, retreats, facilitates workshops and also shares the faith publicly on his faith-based Instagram account Catholicfire_.

This book is his first attempt at documenting his journey and experiences in detail with the hope of providing enlightenment, encouragement and transformation to the reader. In an increasingly secular society where it is widely becoming offensive to speak about religion, faith or spirituality, this book attempts to provide the reader with assurance that we are not meant to passively live our faith behind closed doors; rather we are called to actively and passionately live it to the end just as the apostles and early church fathers.

DEDICATION

I dedicate this book firstly to my Lord and Saviour Jesus Christ who snatched me from the destructive path I was on and guided me towards the path to life. He has blessed me with so much; no amount of gratitude, praise or worship will be enough. I have experienced his love countless times in a very real and tangible way and this book is merely a fragment of the remarkable wonders he has worked in my life.

To my grandmother Monica Brown: just as St. Monica prayed for years for her beloved son St. Augustine, so too, my grandmother prayed earnestly for years for my conversion as I would come to learn. The faith she instilled in me over the years has proven to be invaluable and led me precisely to the place I am today. I am eternally grateful for her guidance and wisdom upon my life.

To my mother Giselle Brown: thank you for taking up the spiritual mantle in the household in recent years and for the support you have given me in every dream I ever decided to chase. I thank you for believing in me continuously when I didn't believe in myself, the consistent reminders of my potential and to not settle for anything less than my best, and the tremendous sacrifices made over the years to allow me to have the opportunities and experiences that I have had to this day.

To my spiritual Father, Fr. Ian Taylor: thank you for the spiritual wisdom and counsel that has been provided over the past decade. I was thrown into the sea of the faith and forced to learn to swim. If it were not for your insight, discernment and trust in me, I could never have gained the wisdom, harnessed the gifts, forged the relationships and experienced all that I have, and I am truly grateful.

It is my hope that this book would be a book that I would have been grateful to receive at some point in my journey and I pray that it can inspire, encourage, and motivate someone at any point in their journey to serve God, not half-heartedly but with everything that they have, because he has given us everything he had to give us through his son Jesus and the Holy Spirit.

PROLOGUE

The love I have received from Jesus Christ has been inexplicable, to say the least. Although my journey has been incredibly fulfilling, it has been equally challenging to the point where nothing else could be relied on but faith. As I reflect, though, I would not trade this journey for anything as I have seen that what the world has to offer is but a shadow of what is found in the all-encompassing and tremendous love of our Lord and Saviour Jesus Christ and I do not mean that in the cliché, anecdotal sense of the phrase, it is something I truly believe. I must, however, add the following caveat: I do not write from a vantage point of theological professionalism, neither do I boast of any philosophical qualifications. There are those who are qualified as such who may do a far better job at expounding on specific scriptures, points and biblical references in this book. I merely write of how God has moved in a mighty way in my life in the last ten years and how the Holy Spirit and scripture speak to me and have completely transformed my identity, outlook and perspective.

In a sense, I feel very much filled with the same conviction and boldness that the apostles received in Acts chapter 2 at Pentecost. This is not a theological book; it is a book to bring to life the very real impact Jesus and his Holy Spirit can have on our lives if we are willing and open to receive. It is my hope that the writings in this book will give hope to you, the reader to overcome the many obstacles that life presents. The avid Christian apologist C.S Lewis highlights in his book "The Problem of Pain" that God allows suffering in this life with sprinkles of joy to remind us that perpetual joy is not to be found here, since this world is not our home.

This theme of the temporality of our lives and everything around us is a recurring theme in this book mainly because I believe it is a concept from which we have become far removed in a society which heavily promotes earthly satisfaction and concupiscence.

The apostles and fathers of the faith understood quite clearly that this faith was more than just words, it involved the giving of everything one had including one's own life when necessary. What moves a man to believe in someone despite suffering, persecution and death itself? For believing in Jesus, the apostles had nothing to gain in this world but ridicule, and they had everything to lose, yet they committed fully to spreading his name and his message to the ends of the earth for the rest of their lives. Why? Were they insane or did some life changing event take place personally in each of their lives that indicated to them that there was something more to life that everyone needed to know? I propose the latter because I have experienced the latter. I have experienced this life changing event: the realization and conviction that life is more than trials, earning a salary, obtaining material comforts and dying.

It is by their example and fervor that we have the most priceless opportunity. If we could earnestly try to wrap our brains around the vastness and sheer sublimity of eternity and the fact that a creator, perfect in nature, would leave his divinity, suffer, die and rise from the dead out of love for you and me so that we too may share in his divine life, then we would realize that believing, living and sharing this message is in fact the most important decision that we will ever make.

I would like to propose based on my own experience that the belief in a God that loves, despite every single fault of ours, despite the times we have rejected his will and pursued our own, despite the number of times we have refused his mercy and still feel his presence yearning upon our hearts, is a love that transcends the understanding many of us have of the word "love". I know that what the apostles and saints have experienced is not mere lunacy as there had been too many opportunities for them to renounce the faith out of persecution and they chose not to. It serves to testify to the fact that we do not ever encounter Jesus and remain the same. If we do, we have not in fact encountered him. Peter was transformed from a timid fisherman to preaching to crowds of thousands and convicting hearts and souls. Paul was transformed from being a murderer of Christians to arguably the greatest writer and evangelist of the New Testament. David was transformed from an adulterer and a murderer to a powerful man after God's heart. Augustine lived a sinful, carefree life of sexual sin and was transformed into one of the most revered bishops and doctors of the church today!

The greatest of saints often start their journey as the greatest of sinners. The message to be realized here is that it matters not how we start, for our future is limitless once we allow ourselves to be *fully* used by God. A close friend of mine, Artherly Nicholas, told me in a conversation once "There is no limit what God can do with you once you are fully open to him." I didn't understand that statement fully until I closely observed how he worshipped God and led others to do so and it inspired me to do the same. It involves a complete abandonment of everything that we hold on to. We become incredibly powerful when we surrender all of our emotions, fears and who we are completely to God because then we become a transparent vessel radiating God's infinite power and love. A love that transforms hearts and triggers a response in return.

This is the standard to which Christ calls us. He raises the bar. The gospel of Matthew 5:43 tells us "You have heard that it was said, 'Love your neighbour and hate your enemy.' But I tell you, love your enemies and pray for those who persecute you." This was the example Jesus himself set and the blessed saints who followed his teachings. Consider how contradictory this must have sounded to a Jewish audience who had been taught the law of Moses of an eye for an eye and repaying evil with evil. Jesus comes along and pushes the Jewish people to transcend what they were taught, that life is not about revenge but about rising above the external impulse to respond and to show mercy. In a sense, all of Jesus' teachings were both transcendent and transformative. He took the entire Old Testament and raised it to a seemingly unimaginable level with unparalleled authority and boldness. This is what separates the figure of Jesus from other religious figureheads. Muhammad, Guatama Buddha and other religious leaders all claimed to know the way to God or eternal bliss; Jesus specifically stated he was The Way (John 14:6) and equated himself to God the Father (John 10:30) and went even further by forgiving sin, setting him apart distinctly from any other historical religious figure. The renowned Christian apologist Ravi Zacharias says that most pose the question "Aren't the world's religions fundamentally the same?" He goes on to explain, however, that the question is misplaced, "the world's religions are fundamentally different and at best superficially similar." Once we understand the exclusive nature of Christianity, the person who Jesus claimed to be and the hundreds of prophecies of his birth, death and resurrection that he accurately fulfilled, we recognize that no one else in human history fits this mold. Only then may we start to comprehend the intensity of the passion of serving Christ which the saints emanated. Some examples are highlighted below:

St. Ignatius of Antioch upon being fed to lions for his belief in Christ is quoted as saying, "I prefer death in Christ Jesus to power over the farthest limits of the earth. He who died in place of us is the one object of my quest. He who rose for our sakes is my one desire."

St. Stephen upon being stoned to death said "Lord Jesus welcome me....forgive them for they know not what they do."

St. Polycarp the last living apostle of the gospel writer John, upon being convinced to renounce Jesus by threat of burning to death as well as being fed to wild animals, replied in his old age "Eighty six years I have served him and he has done me no wrong. How can I blaspheme my King and Saviour?"

St. Maximilian Kolbe was a Polish priest who died as prisoner 16770 in Auschwitz, on August 14, 1941. When a prisoner escaped from the camp, the Nazis selected ten others to be killed by starvation in reprisal for the escape. One of the ten selected to die, Franciszek Gajowniczek, began to cry: "My wife! My children! I will never see them again!" At this, Maximilian Kolbe stepped forward and asked to die in his place. His request was granted. He was later canonized in the year 1982 by Pope John Paul II.

These saints all embraced God's call upon their lives and followed that call until the very end. Have we? God calls each of us; unfortunately many of us do not hear the call because of the noise of the world. This is the challenge. It matters not how we start, but it is critical how we end as our eternity is dependent on it. Let us challenge ourselves, then, to quiet our hearts and hear the call. The past decade has given us a plethora of distractions to take us away from the voice of the creator. The internet and social media have become our voices in today's world, so much so that many of us seem far removed from the burning love of the saints throughout the ages. We are all called, however, to have the burning desire which the saints and apostles personified. If God's promise of his resurrection is true, so too is the promise of his Holy Spirit to be with us until the end of time. Jesus knew we could not make it to the end on our own, he knew our zeal would be exhausted and our hope would fade, so he left his advocate to be with us to the very end. It is the spirit who convicts, the spirit drowns out the voice of the world, the spirit creates that fire within us to serve. He comforts us in our time of affliction, advises us in time of uncertainty, renews us in times of spiritual drought. It is the spirit then, whom we must rely on to speak to us through the word of God. It is this same spirit I rely on as I write.

The book will highlight various scriptures from both the New and Old Testament that are explained in the context of practical examples, my own life's testimonies and today's world events, in the hope of providing encouragement, a different perspective on undergoing trials and renewed life to the reader. It focuses on seven particular elements: Suffering, Love, Identity, Perspective, Victory, Being a Witness and finally, Purpose. I must reiterate, these were not chosen based on any theological underpinnings. I am aware that differences of doctrine exist among the different Christian faiths and this is not a book that will pursue doctrinal or religious debates. That may be a future project.

This is, however, a book which has used these seven topics as pillars for discussion as they have been glaring signposts on my own journey as a charismatic Catholic Christian and have led me to live victoriously in Christ. It also provides an insight into the person of Jesus Christ and why believing in him adequately equips us to face the many trials that this life may bring.

Scriptures are taken from the New Jerusalem Bible. They are not designed to be read in any particular order. It can be read chronologically or at random, but I pray wherever God guides you to start, that He may be the one speaking to you through the pages. Happy reading!

SUFFERING

You might be wondering here why kick start a book of encouragement with a discussion on suffering. Truth be told, I started writing this book in December 2017, at quite a dark point in my life where I was consumed with brokenness and depression. Even though I knew God and had a relationship with Jesus, I had to cry out to him continuously to restore my faith and gain a semblance of peace. I started writing a journal of my emotions since I felt I couldn't relay how I was feeling to many people, mostly because I felt I was the one who usually helped people in my various social circles and that sharing weak moments would diminish my ability to do so. Thankfully, I have come to view that differently, recognizing that it was in fact a bit of pride I needed to shed and realizing that all of us are in need of God's grace and help from each other in some way.

Reading what I wrote disturbed me. It didn't sound like words of a believer, rather it sounded like someone who had lost hope. I thought to myself, if I was walking with Christ and felt this way, how many more would be going through similar experiences and not speaking about it. God then placed a call upon my heart to start formalizing my writing. Through the writings came healing and he started revealing people in my life who needed the very lessons that he was teaching me. So I start with suffering because this is where the journey started with me. I pray that the Holy Spirit will move through the words as you read.

I will now explore the concept of suffering in the context of a few key scriptures that the Holy Spirit has prompted for use:

Suffering is indeed a phenomenon which engages the full cadre of negative emotions: pain, anger, confusion, disappointment, jealousy, bitterness. Nothing reminds us of our humanity more than the sufferings we endure throughout this life and none of us are exempt. It is not dependent on class, race or creed. Often times we feel helpless and hopeless to the immense pressure that the troubles of this world can bring. This pressure can be unbearable and relentless, however I propose that if God chose suffering as the method through which salvation came into the world, we must concede that there has to be some merit in the spiritual transformation that it allows us to undergo and that merit is worth examining.

In suffering, we are reduced. Usually we go through some form of physical, emotional or mental loss or situations simply just do not work out in our favour. There is no shortage of these examples in this life: death, financial difficulty, divorce, betrayal, rape, corruption, sickness, starvation; the list can seem endless. Many times we need to be shattered for us to realize how self-sufficient we thought we were. Suffering is also a potent reminder of the lack of priority that we give to God, not because of his proud desire for us to worship him as an omnipotent being in need of our praise in some way, but to remind us that we are in need of his love and are incomplete without it. We often only run to God earnestly and fall on our knees in desperation, when all other options are exhausted. This is not the relationship that God desires to have with us. He should not be our last resort; in fact it should be quite the opposite. Our relationship with him should be so pervasive that he is the first person we speak to in any situation, good or bad because he ultimately knows and wants what is best for us. Quite often though we fail at this. We are excellent at giving him praise and thanks when things are good but we are quick to blame him when things go contrary to our expectations. God however did not change, even though our situation did. If God loved you enough to give you the son you prayed for after many years of trying, he will also be the God to supply your needs to take care of that same son. He is constant in his love for us but we often allow the situations in our life to be overly magnified and take precedence over the relationship with him because the relationship is in fact frail.

If our relationship with him were potent, we would understand quite clearly how much he loves us in the midst of our pain and how much he wants to free and deliver us from what may seem to us like a dire situation. Sadly, for so many of us, it is not until things we hold dear to us are stripped away do we understand that this is the person who was meant to fill the perpetual ache and void that we all feel inside.

Another point worth considering is that God always operates with our eternity in mind; we unfortunately do not. Consider the following example of the king and the mansion. There is a king who lives in a beautiful mansion with his beloved son. Within the mansion there are dozens of rooms each with a different delight for the enjoyment of his son but the son has one toy car which he loves, so much so that he would simply stay in his room all day and play with his toy.

Seeing this, one day the king decides to hide the toy while the son sleeps, knowing that if only he would come out of the closet, he would see the beauty of the room and if only he would leave the room, he would see the beauty of the mansion and be infinitely more satisfied. So while the child sleeps, the king hides the toy. The child wakes up, looks for the toy, doesn't find it and is devastated. The king sees the child crying and is saddened initially because his son is in pain but in his wisdom, he knows that his pain is temporary. Soon enough the child comes out of the room and stops crying. He sees other rooms, filled with so many other toys that he had never seen and he is shocked at first then filled with joy! The father looks on at the son's joy and is pleased. He knows that he made the right decision.

Many of us are like that little child. We are crying over our hidden toy. The toy which we loved. The toy which meant everything to us. We did not know that there were bigger, better toys awaiting us. We didn't know that there were other rooms with toys that we had never seen that would give us delight that we never imagined. Instead we cried over our lost toy in sorrow even asking God to replace it. We were blinded by what seemed to be the only good thing we would ever have in our life and could not imagine a life without that 'thing' once it was removed.

This simple story is analogous to the sublime wisdom God exhibits in our lives. We are all that child at different times in our lives and if we never come out of the *bedrooms* of our lives we will never see what lies ahead. What often happens though is because we can be so obstinate in our resolve, God, like the king in the story will often hide or even destroy 'our toy' for us to see that there is beauty beyond the present - beauty we never imagined. He knows that it will cause us some temporary discomfort which actually saddens him as well because like any father he is in touch with the emotions of his children, but in his wisdom he knows it is for our greater good.

We must believe in the wisdom of our father. We must have the assurance that he will always act in our best interest whether this means gaining or losing things in this life. It is all for our good, good meaning our salvation. We must rely on his spirit to trust his wisdom despite the pain in the present moment. He knows better. Let us swallow the pride, limit the tears and receive the joy. We must be willing, though, to rise above our emotions and our proclivity to trust in ourselves to provide our own joy. We must recognize that while it may satisfy, it is transitory, and the only place we are ever completely joyful is in Christ.

If anyone wants to be a follower of mine, let him renounce himself and take up his cross every day and follow me. Luke 9:23

In the past few decades there has been a surge in the preaching of what is now termed 'prosperity gospels'. The name relates to its focus on the aspects of God's word which talk about our well-being and improving our current material state. It should be no surprise then that many of these preachers have churches whose congregations number in the tens of thousands. Can we really blame them though? The answer in my opinion is two-fold. 'No', from the perspective of we all prefer to hear good news as opposed to bad. If someone were to tell us today that we were to win a jackpot, we would be infinitely more elated than if they told us that we had to sacrifice our first born son for such a jackpot. Within our design is the innate desire for pleasure and satisfaction and our preferences and daily choices indicate such. However, the answer to the question of blame is also 'Yes', because we as Christians (preachers and receivers) have a responsibility to equip ourselves with the fullness of truth within God's word. To preach a unilateral message of blessings and omit suffering or the "difficult" scriptures is disingenuous and a watered down message of truth.

We must understand clearly that only the fullness of truth saves. Within this truth, God designed that there were lessons and revelations that would only be gained through suffering, a suffering from which he did not even spare his own son. To preach a message of prosperity and blessings only is actually 'Anti-Christ' in nature since it is contrary to the very teachings of Jesus. It does not equip the faithful to be prepared for the trials of life which *will* come. There is no safe place we can flee to be trial-free, in this world.

I would like to be very clear though, it is not that God has meant for us to only suffer in this life as there are many beautiful aspects of our life to appreciate and he wants us to fully enjoy the awe and splendor of his creation. However, he also wants us to be fully equipped to deal with the many temptations and sorrows that will come since he knows our fragile nature and the deceptions of this world.

It would be the equivalent of giving a homeless drug addict a few hundred thousand dollars to improve his life. Without the proper financial wisdom to use the money wisely, the blessing may be more of a curse since the individual would now have a greater avenue to facilitate his destructive habit. The point here is that God does not only want to bless us materially, even though this is what most of us may want. He wants to shape, transform and ultimately perfect us for what awaits us, which is the perfect act of love. Love ultimately transforms us into the people we need to be, so essentially when we ask for God to *only* bless us we are ultimately asking him to love us less not more. We are asking him to give us the bag of money without the wisdom and fortitude to use it for our good. Let us learn to embrace the lessons saints!

Why would God choose suffering as the means through which redemption came into the world?

The fact is this, I do not know. I cannot God prescribe why God chose suffering as the way to shape us within this life but I can say the following. I know for certainty the decision to allow it is not without merit. I have personally suffered horrific circumstances within my own life and questioned God many times as to why he would allow certain things to occur (which I will discuss in a later chapter). With the passage of time I eventually realized how much I was transformed from enduring the particular circumstance. It is similar to a child trying to understand a manner of punishment that a parent will elicit. A child may be told he is under punishment and cannot go outside to play. Through the lens of a child this is a traumatic experience, but through the lens of the parent it is an opportunity for discipline to be taught because the parent understands that discipline is a necessary trait for life. We will not understand the lesson until we become adults or even parents ourselves and wear the same lens.

Similarly, when we ask questions that start with "Why would God....." our problem is the fact that we are trying to see an eternal outcome through an earthly lens. Through our lens, our situations are tragic, horrific, such as the murder of a parent or child. Horrific as it may be to us, we must bear in mind that God operates with less of our current emotions and more of our eternal salvation in mind. We often accuse an eternal God of making bad temporal decisions, having no real idea of a concept of eternity ourselves. How do you even start explaining something infinite when the very tool used to do the explanation (*your brain*) is finite? All we have and will ever have are at best, estimations, but we will never fully grasp the lessons to be learned until we wear his lens when we enter into divinity.

We have available to us our present moment and our past, as much as our memory will allow. God sees our past, present and future available to us in a perpetually present moment. If something occurs in our present moment which we may not like, but it equips and transforms us into being more Christ-like, who are we to judge the event as '*bad*'. We are not merely called to worship Christ but to be like him and unfortunately that means walking the path that he walked: suffering unto glory. As this book highlights, the good news for us is that we are given clear glimpses of his lens and eternity through his word, his Holy Spirit and the ministry of his Church and only by wholly immersing ourselves in these elements consistently do we become adequately equipped to see suffering for what it is and learn the relevant and necessary lessons to be the people that God has called us to be.

Unload all your burden on to him, since he is concerned about you. 1 Peter 5:7

If we are honest with ourselves, there are many things that break and crush our spirit in this life. We are sometimes tempted to say that God is perfect and does not understand how we feel but I propose differently because he proposes differently. It is in these critical moments, we must understand that our Lord experienced exactly what we have been through. He does not speak from a place of perfection in heaven, distant from our trials. He knows our pain intimately, because he knows *us* intimately which is why he can say he cares for us. It is said that the suffering that Jesus underwent at his crucifixion was the most complete and extreme suffering one could experience. It was in fact so painful that the word "excruciating" was created to describe it. Literally meaning "out of the cross".

Physical Suffering - The cross Jesus carried was said to have weighed close to 300 lbs. The total distance from Gethsemane to Calvary was about 1.5 kilometers, almost four laps around an Olympic sized track. Consider also, that the cross was carried uphill after he was thoroughly scourged with sharp pieces of metal designed to tear flesh from the bone causing the most unimaginable human torture. He also had sharp thorns twisted into a crown and pierced into his scalp. At the end of the journey, his shoulder had to be pulled out of place so that he could be nailed to the cross through his wrists and feet. Crucifixion was also meant to inflict maximum suffering as the victims would have to hold their entire body weight up by the wounds. This made it increasingly difficult to breathe. Every breath was a life draining effort until the victim died from asphyxia.

Social Humiliation - He also suffered the public embarrassment of being perched naked on top of Calvary Hill, in hypothermic temperatures and subjected to insults and curses from the very people who welcomed him into Jerusalem one week earlier.

Emotional/Spiritual Suffering - Aside from the physical torture, Jesus underwent tremendous spiritual agony as he would soon be forsaken for a time by the Father and undergo a literal experience of Hell before conquering death through the resurrection. The magnitude of taking the sins of the entire world upon himself coupled with feeling abandoned by not only his apostles but his own Father gripped Jesus in the garden and caused him great distress. This is clearly seen when he utters the words "Father, if you are willing, take this cup from me; yet not my will, but yours be done" Luke 22:42. The weight of the task before him was so ominous that Jesus begged the Father for a way out; his humanity in this moment was shown. He suffered emotionally, he felt abandoned, betrayed and alone, and he also faced the mammoth of all capital punishments for crimes of which he was falsely accused. The lesson, however, is that in the face of all of this tragedy, he was still able to find the hope to believe in the Father's will over his own.

It is difficult to imagine being in the shoes of Jesus in these moments but we can think of moments of betrayal in our own lives. We can think of moments where we were falsely accused, where we were publicly shamed, where we underwent tremendous emotional or physical suffering for something that had nothing to do with us. Suddenly, we see a God who is not sitting afar looking down on us, rather we see a God who is very closely intertwined in our situations because having gone through the most complete suffering, he alone understands *exactly* what we feel. This is why Peter tells us that Jesus cares for us. He cares because he knows the feeling of betrayal and he knows suffering because he lived it.

I have drawn upon the suffering of Jesus to illustrate that even in his perfection, he endured the same human weaknesses as we did in every way, except he did not sin. This, then, is the blueprint that we are called to follow. Every time Jesus felt overwhelmed by the weight of his suffering, he had a particular response. He turned to his heavenly father for strength knowing that he could not endure the journey alone. This is precisely the manner in which we must handle the trials that we face in our daily lives. The ego tells us "You're strong enough to deal with this on your own" or "Don't show your pain, you're a man" but God did not design us to carry the weight of the trials of this world on our own. Every one of us has our breaking point, that limit where we throw our hands up in the air with the realization that we just do not have the answer or the strength.

Sooner or later many of us come to the realization that we were made with a longing for supernatural strength that only he can provide. He knew that there would be times that we would need help to deal with the massive hurt caused by the circumstances of this life. With Jesus as the example, let us forsake our pride and be humble enough to admit that God is there for us. God is relatable to us and through him we have the victory. The enemy wants us to believe that we are strong or wise enough when in fact he is far stronger and wiser than we are, on our own. He is cunning and will convince us of a false reality if we are not attentive to the voice of God in our lives. Let us then submit wholly to the voice of God, giving all situations to him as he told us. Only then will we truly be at peace and understand the maxim as stated by the avid apologist C.S Lewis: "If I find in myself desires which nothing in this world can satisfy, the only logical explanation is that I was made for another world."

So God said to Noah, I have decided that the end has come for all living things, for the earth is full of lawlessness because of human beings. So I am now about to destroy them and the earth. Make yourself an ark out of resinous wood. Make it of reeds and caulk it with pitch inside and out. This is how to make it: the length of the ark is to be three hundred cubits, its breadth fifty cubits, and its height thirty cubits. Make a roof to the ark, building it up to a cubit higher. Put the entrance in the side of the ark, which is to be made with lower, second and third decks. Genesis 6:13-16

The story of Noah is undoubtedly one of the most popular stories of the Bible and of Christian households. In a nutshell, God becomes incredibly displeased with the sin of mankind and decides to destroy all creation on earth except one righteous family and the animals brought into the ark.

The aspect of the story I want to focus on however is not on God's wrath as is commonly discussed but on the time Noah took to prepare for the impending disaster. Noah didn't wait until the rain came to start building the ark. What does this mean for us?

Many of us suffer in life, but many of us are also frequently ill-prepared to deal with the sufferings that we undergo because we do not allow ourselves the time to be prepared or strengthened. I acknowledge that there may be tragic circumstances that one can never fully be ready for, but there are also many circumstances where we have the opportunity to be adequately prepared if we are attentive to the manner in which our lives unfold. He opens our eyes, he prepares us, and just like with Noah, he tells us exactly what we need to do to navigate through the storm, once we are willing. God advised Noah on the specific preparation he needed to undergo to avoid the impending disaster and Noah listened. Foolish as he seemed in the sight of everyone else, Noah obeyed even when that meant building an ark on dry land without a single drop of rain in sight. The point here is that regardless of the impending disaster that may come our way, when we listen to the voice of God in our lives we can usually recognize a season of preparation. Then we become adequately equipped to sustain, endure and overcome.

God will often speak to us and warn us, but we may refuse to see the signs. He may be closing doors all around us that we may insist on walking through. Similarly he may be calling us to do something that we think is impossible. Something that may be radically different from the societal norm but rest assured, God does not fit into our little box of expectation.

We ought not to rule out any idea as too crazy, irrational or difficult for God to demand of us. If he asks much of you it is because he expects much from you and will empower you to do exactly what he asks.

We must understand, though, the importance of timing. Procrastination has a consequence! Had Noah started to build the ark when the rain started to fall, he would have been destroyed with everyone else. It is therefore critical that we recognize our season of preparation since it may be too late for us later on. An athlete does not start training for a race the day before. It takes months and sometimes years of discipline, dedication and commitment to compete for ten seconds of glory but successful athletes know that this is what is required. Do we however, as budding saints, running an eternal race, know what is required? We need to be even more committed, prepared and focused on the eternal prize in front of us for if we miss our time of preparation and training, we do not get a chance to run another race. Let us listen, be astute and obedient, let us run well.

PERSONAL TESTIMONY

I do not speak of suffering from a distant place. I do not speak of it as some abstract concept to give persons false hope. I speak of the reality of suffering because I have lived it and I speak of the reality of his love because I have come to experience this personally. As I share below on my own journey, I urge you to read with an understanding that the God I serve would not only deliver me from the dark abyss of tragedy and hurt that I was in but he can and will deliver you too! Let's go!

The experiences in my life have taught me that our faith can run on autopilot for a significant period of time before a particular moment ignites our relationship with Jesus. For many years, this was my life.

I was born in the small Caribbean twin island of Trinidad and Tobago, into a staunch Catholic family with a grandmother who firmly believed in Jesus Christ and imparted that same faith to the entire family. However, as the old adage goes, you can lead a horse to the well but you cannot force it to drink. Children can be fed all the healthy food required, but with time, junk food always seems more enticing. It is the same with our faith. My grandmother spent tremendous time praying for my family and I for many years but for quite a long time I preferred junk instead of the substance of faith that I was taught. Faith seemed something necessary as a child but as life progressed, its importance seemed to fade. However, God's plan was greater. I attended a Catholic primary school and one of my fondest memories was sitting in our front porch with my grandmother, learning various psalms of the bible during summer vacation. I remember all the prayers that I was taught; they lived within me as I grew.

I then moved on successfully to St. Mary's College, another Catholic school, although sadly this didn't do much for my faith. As I got older, the voice of peers started to take precedence over the voice of God instilled in me over the years and very soon doing what was popular took precedence over doing what was right. For years this would be the case, as my behavior mirrored those around me and I became the token 'follower of the crowd'.

My father who had been absent for most of my childhood, made guest appearances every now and then in my life. Although he lived in New York, he managed to keep in contact with me via telephone and letters over the years. I didn't have the closest relationship with him but I think I loved him because I knew I was supposed to. I remember meeting him for the first time when I was ten years old. My mom and I visited him in New York and I remember seeing him in JFK airport running up to us. I thought to myself 'Wow, he has really small ears'. It is now a light memory which still puts a smile on my face. Although he was around when I was born, he left when I was three years old so I had no memory of him before this first visit to New York at the age of ten. It still remains to this day, memories that have been etched onto my heart. We immediately hit it off, played basketball together, went to the malls and had father-son conversations for the first time. It was as if I found a part of me that had been missing and leaving him after three weeks was literally one of the hardest things I ever had to do. I remember him telling me he loved me and that he would see me soon, a bitter sweet moment before my return home to Trinidad.

I would visit again at the age of fourteen and the spark would reignite again. The reminder that I had a father that was there for me was a foreign joy to which I was starting to get accustomed. The trip was similar but this time there were conversations about relationships and women since I was getting a bit older; awkward, to say the least but noteworthy as it would stay with me until my adult life. I remember one day while sitting in the living room of his apartment, he asked me in front of my mother "So Jameke, you having sex?" Although I wasn't, the question raised every hair on my body and sent shockwaves through me as this was not a topic of conversation I ever had in front of any parent before. I managed to distract myself with a movie and prayed that the inquisition would be over. Thankfully, my discomfort possibly showed him I was not ready for those things and he ended the questioning.

Upon my return to Trinidad this time though, things were different. After a few months, the calls and the letters stopped, and before the age of social media, it was quite difficult to maintain an overseas relationship without phone calls or letters. Months turned into a year and I had not heard from him and I began asking my mom questions. Her response would always be something to the effect of "He's busy" or "He's at work" but something inside of me knew something was wrong. Thankfully at this time I was writing CXC examinations so I had something else to occupy my attention. It was not until the age of sixteen things would start making sense again. I remember vividly one day my mother pulled me aside to talk to me. She told me "Your dad is coming back to Trinidad to live". To date, I cannot adequately articulate the emotion I felt at that point. It was a mixture of confusion, anxiety and joy. Confusion because I had not heard from him in almost two years, anxiety because I couldn't wait to see him and joy because of how much I had missed him. I spent those days before his coming in great anticipation and excitement. I thought about how my friends would refer to their families and about the things they would do with their fathers and the thought that I would finally have that gave me great peace inside. I was also at that age where boys wanted to be and act much older than they were so I wanted to be just like him, dress like him and act like him.

I remember seeing him finally for the first time after those two years. What a feeling of completion to know that he would now be back home with me permanently.

This however did not nullify the fact that I was left with many unanswered questions, the main one being his absence and lack of communication over the last two years. I waited until the time was right when we got home and I asked him. I could see his face change from the peace of being with his son to a look of disappointment. He then proceeded to tell me "Jameke I was locked up for the past year and when I came out they deported me to Trinidad." I couldn't process it all in that moment but I remember feeling a wave of sadness come over me. It was as if the version of the father I knew now became replaced with that of a criminal in an instant and it hurt. I took some time to wrap my mind around it. He went on to explain that he was falsely imprisoned and the whole thing was a mistake. Whether it was true or not, now I'll never know, but it's what he told me as a teenager and his is the only version of the story to which I have been privy.

After some time we managed to change the topic and soon we started making the most of every day. I would visit him daily after school and spend all my time at his home. We talked a lot about many different things: life, respecting others, finances, manners, he even gave me advice on relationships and intimacy. It was new to me. We had talked in previous years but I could tell now he was treating me as someone older and I appreciated that. He also told me to always be there for my two younger sisters, and even though these were not my mother's children, I still loved them and made a decision that I would. It almost felt like he was subtly passing a mantle on to me. Little did I know how much those conversations would prepare me for what I was about to face.

<u>January 21st, 2007</u>

It was now the third week since he had returned and things were going quite well, at least through my eyes. Looking back now as an adult, I can't imagine how difficult it must have been for him. He had built a life in New York for over twelve years and now he was sent back to Trinidad with nothing and forced to start over. However, through the eyes of a sixteen year old, coupled with the fact that he hid his emotions well, I would've never imagined at that point how challenging it must have all been for him. I remember that particular Sunday, January 21st, 2007, I spent the entire day with him. He cooked grilled fish and potatoes. I was not a fan of fish, but he made it so I ate and enjoyed. Being out of my comfort zone never seemed to be a problem once I was in his presence. I remember one conversation specifically where he reminded me of how proud he was of me and that I would do things that he never did. He told me to strive for excellence and be the best at what I do and reminded me of how much my mother and grandmother had done for me. These words didn't have much meaning to me until later on. That day would turn out to be one of the most important and memorable days in my life for several reasons.

My parents lived in separate homes so my mother came to pick me up in the evening as I had school the next day. I encouraged my dad to come along for the drive just so I could have some more time with him. I didn't even consider the fact that this would mean my mother would have to drop him back home then return to our home by herself late at night. Again my age made me relatively oblivious to such factors. God however, would allow things to unfold this way for a reason. Before leaving he asked if he could borrow my PlayStation. Of course I was most willing but remembered that I had lent it to my neighbour. Casually I said to him "Don't worry, you'll get it tomorrow, one day wouldn't kill you." I proceeded inside and headed to bed and my mom returned to drop him home.

Two hours later I jumped up from my sleep, as my cell phone rang. It was my cousin.
"Jameke, Jameke, where's your dad, I'm trying to call him and he's not answering!" she exclaimed.
"Umm he's supposed to be at home", I answered, "my mom brought him back home."
"Ok", she replied and hung up.

It was absolutely the strangest conversation ever because so many things did not make sense. My cousin and my dad lived in the same house; this was his brother's daughter. I could not comprehend why she would be calling me to find out where my dad was. Secondly, I thought to myself why didn't she simply call his cell phone? However being awakened from sleep, I did not have the most coherent thoughts about the events of that night. I simply provided a brief answer and returned to sleep.

I got up the next morning and looked at my phone. I realized it was 7:00 am. No one woke me up for school and I was now late. This was strange since if I did not hear my alarm, my grandmother would usually wake me. I jumped out of bed and hurried to the bathroom. Unknowingly I passed both my mother and grandmother sitting in my mother's bedroom, completely overlooking the fact that my mother was present and not at work. As I headed back to my room I noticed them. My mother was sitting on her bed and my grandmother on a chair by the door. Nothing about the scene was right. So I immediately asked my mother the most obvious question, "Why aren't you at work today and umm… how come no one woke me up for school?" I had not yet made eye contact with either of them, I was so busy thinking about the fact that I was late. It was then I looked up and noticed my mother's face. Her eyes were red and swollen as if she had been crying but deeper than that she had a look on her face that I never saw before. One of absolute despair. This immediately snapped me out of my preoccupations and brought me into the reality of the moment. I looked at my grandmother, the rock, the beacon of strength hoping to find comfort in her eyes but she looked incredibly filled with sorrow and compassion also and this deeply bothered me. Afraid to ask much, I simply muttered, "What happened?"

"Jameke you should come and sit down" she replied. I didn't, and I asked again, "What happened? Why are you crying?" At this point I knew that what I was about to hear would be something for which I was not prepared because I had never seen strength escape both my mother and grandmother simultaneously in a situation before.

"It's your dad they shot him" she said.

I felt a piece of my soul break a bit, but still filling myself with immediate reassurance I proceeded to ask "Where is he? Is he at the hospital? Is he ok?" With tears running down her face she then said the words that changed my life forever, "He died."

Everything suddenly went numb and in an instant the pain flooded in, "What?!!!! He's dead??? How can this happen??!!!" Tears poured down my face as I fell to the ground. My grandmother held me to offer some comfort but I did not want it. I stormed out of the room, slammed the door and started smashing and breaking things in my room. I was absolutely broken and confused that God would take my father away from me especially in such a tragic manner as this. I could not rationalize it and it was just too much for me. My uncles tried comforting me and telling me that it would be okay but I didn't want to hear any of it. Memories of just a few hours before filled my mind - How much we talked, laughed and had a good time - and to think that someone took that away from me angered me and lit a fire inside of me. I also remembered the last words I ever told him "Don't worry, you'll get it tomorrow, one day wouldn't kill you" and how I took life for granted. It was truly devastating and an incredibly chaotic scene. Crying all around, hopelessness, despair. I had no idea how to start processing something like this. I had never dealt with death in such an intimate way before. I didn't know what to do, what to think, how to feel, I just knew what I felt was complete emptiness and nothing made it feel better. No conversations, no meals, no hobbies, it was simply a sadness that was debilitating and it is truly something I wish no one ever had to experience. All of life's worst emotions were visibly present in our home that day and it was an absolute mess.

In the next few months, my grandmother would be the voice of wisdom in my life as she had always been. Even though I did not always want to hear her words, she persisted and ensured that she did her part in providing me with the shoulder that I needed and the words of comfort and support at that time and I remain eternally grateful for it. In the months that followed I would spend a lot of time talking with her. She would often tell me that God works in mysterious ways and that everything happens for a reason but this did not offer much hope for me to hold on to as I did not yet have a personal relationship with Jesus to understand on my own. Nevertheless, I trusted her and I valued her opinion. So even though I did not believe everything she told me at that point, I listened.

About six months passed and I was starting to come along slowly. I still felt like a part of me was missing but I managed to find some semblance of happiness at times with friends either playing tennis or PlayStation or something to take my mind off the loss. I had also started considering that maybe this did happen for a reason that one day maybe in the very distant future I would understand. Things were seemingly headed in the right direction, but I was not prepared for the next chapter.

One day while walking home from school, one neighbor stopped me to talk to me.
"Hey Jameke, how are you?"
"Good, good" I replied.
"How have you been? I heard about your dad." He asked.
Not really being a mood to elaborate, I said "Well, I'm coming along."
He then asked a question that would turn my entire world upside down "And how is your grandmother doing with the cancer?"
Everything around me in that moment went silent as I attempted to process what I had just heard.
"Umm…what???" I responded in disbelief.

Realizing I did not know anything, he attempted to change the topic to football or some other sport and in my not wanting to accept what I just mistakenly heard, I continued talking about sports as if the previous question was never mentioned.

As I walked off though, reality would soon set in and a daunting heaviness came over me. I equated cancer with death. I had heard too many stories of people losing loved ones to the disease and the thought of losing her now became a horrifying reality. My grandmother was the sole voice of peace and reason in my life at this point. I remember talking to God as I continued walking home and eventually the tears started to flow. I thought to myself "How can I live without my grandmother Lord? She is everything to me!"

My mother was still going through a hard time; there were many times she could not hold it together. The thought of losing my grandmother from cancer was not an option in my mind as I felt the entire family would simply break down and become a house of complete sorrow. In a sense, I felt she was needed. I also remember being very angry at the fact that none of them told me about the situation. I felt as if they still viewed me as a child who they had to protect from bad news and this irked me. I decided at that point that I would not say anything about my knowledge of the sickness. I came home that day and prayed and cried. My relationship with God was not the best. I had cursed him many times after 'taking' my father in the manner that he did and I tried not to have to ever really talk to him too much after that. Besides the fact that I did not understand what a relationship with God meant, I simply viewed his existence as a being somewhere out there to assist when we need help. This situation however warranted that help. I knelt down that day by my bed and I pleaded with God in the most candid way.

"God I don't know very much about how you work, but I need you now. My grandmother is sick. She has cancer. I don't know how bad it is but I know what cancer can do. Lord we need her here. She is everything to me. Please heal her. If you heal her, I will believe in you. I will live my life better. I will live for you."

I thought the wager was good enough. I ask for her healing, I serve him in return. Fair game. However, God would flip the script on me and make me realize that he doesn't fit into our little box of bribes and favors. He always operates with eternity in mind, since this is his nature. That being said, I said the prayer and I waited. I tried my best to interact normally with them both but the fact that they were hiding such an important piece of information weighed heavily on me. I would look at my grandmother every day to see if my prayers were being answered. It was now March 2008. I had not seen any improvement. In fact she appeared to be getting worse. She had lost approximately 20-30lbs in the space of three months. It was not apparent to me since I was seeing her every day, coupled with the fact that I believed my mind intentionally overlooked her weight loss because of the subconscious hope that she would be healed. It was not until one afternoon when I came home from school, and I heard loud shrieks piercing the air would I realize the severity of her condition. Her older sister, my great-aunt had come to visit her and she could not stop screaming when she saw my grandmother. She shrieked "She's skin and bones! She's skin and bones!" On this day my grandmother was too weak to talk and breathing was difficult. It boggles my mind to this day that I had become so oblivious to the severity of her condition. I was in denial of the whole thing and very unwilling to accept the situation because I felt I had made a good enough prayer with God. I also felt God owed me. I felt he took my dad, so he needed to repay me and let my grandmother live. Naive to say the least. If only the adult Jameke was around to talk to my seventeen year old self, and impart some wisdom then.

I persevered in prayer nonetheless until one day in May when things took an unexpected and sharp turn for the worst. One day in May, my mother and grandmother had returned home from one of their 'trips' as they would call it and my mother told me she needed to talk to me, so I obliged. I was busy in the kitchen so I did not really make eye contact. When I did, it was déjà vu. I saw the look again. The same look she had right before she gave me the news of my dad's death. The best way I can explain it is that sinking feeling you experience in your stomach when in a moment of real fear. I just felt my stomach sink and I prepared for the worst as I stared into my mother's face of despair.

"Mummy has cancer and the doctors say that there's nothing else they can do, it's just a matter of time now" she said. This time, however, it was different. Although I was broken by this news, I reminded myself that I had prayed for her and I was waiting for God to come through for me. That night I prayed like never before for her healing. Two more months had passed and CAPE exams had begun. I was now in Upper 6 so I knew I had to try to focus on my exams in the midst of all that was going on. Although school was arduous, it provided a bit of a mental break from the stress at home that I had been under.

July 11, 2008

On this particular day I had an Economics exam but due to the amount of family members that had been in our house visiting my grandmother, I did not get the time to study adequately, so I got up at about 3:00am to cram some last minute information for a few hours before the exam. As I would usually do, I checked on my grandmother to make sure she was okay. This time, however, was different, I didn't put on the light. I just passed and held her hand for a few seconds. While holding her hand, I noticed something. Her chest was not moving. I was in shock in this moment but still in denial so I waited because I knew that her breathing had slowed down so I thought this was the case. Five minutes passed and she still had not taken a breath. Ten minutes. Fifteen minutes. Twenty. Twenty-five. Then reality hit me like a brick. I had been holding her hand for almost half hour now and she had not taken a single breath. My denial had blinded me. I refused to see how she had degenerated over the months, the weight she had lost and now I refused to believe that she could possibly be dead in my arms. I shook her hand. I spoke to her.

"Mummy, wake up" "Wake up, please." "Please wake up!" "Please wake up!!" I shook her hand vigorously now, refusing to accept the reality that was before me. I grabbed her other hand. I started speaking to her in an audible voice "Mummy please, please wake up!" I felt hopelessness setting in. I felt the pain of losing my father rushing back in. I felt the hatred towards God rushing back. I felt everything that I had tried to ignore for past few months coming straight towards me head on like a truck. Fearing the worst I ran to my mother and woke her up and told her that my grandmother was not breathing. I could not go back to the bedroom where she was because once my mother got there I knew what would take place. By this time, my uncles were alerted that Mummy was not breathing and we needed to call an ambulance. The ambulance arrived within minutes and after making initial checks confirmed the fears that we all prayed we would never have to hear. Mummy was dead. My rock. My spiritual fortress. My everything. The only place where I felt completely at peace was now taken away from me and that absolutely crushed me. I could not come to terms with it. The facade of strength that I was holding on to in previous months was now stripped away and I let everything out, I could hold it in no longer.

The DMO arrived and placed her in a body bag and it was in that moment I lost it. I felt like if someone had literally taken my heart and stabbed it repeatedly. The pain was so surreal. Worse than the loss of my father because while I had only shared glimpses of happiness with my dad, my grandmother was everything to me since my birth. She took me to school, helped me with homework, taught me how to pray, rewarded me when I did well in exams, encouraged me, supported me and most importantly loved me so much. My life was littered with so many beautiful memories of her and in the time when I needed her the most to help me, she was gone. I could not forgive God for this. I decided I would not and I would now start living and doing things that pleased me.

<u>September 2008</u>

I started my Bachelor's degree in Business Management at the University of the West Indies (UWI). It was now two months since my grandmother had died and the wound was still very fresh and the pain still very real. University, however, was a new experience for me. A new environment, new people, and it offered many distractions to deal with my pain. Soon enough I was fully immersed in this new environment and culture that was UWI. I would soon become involved in many things that university students engage themselves in: frequent parties, alcohol, missing classes and my grades started to suffer. I was also in a relationship at the time which started to suffer due to the many female "distractions" at University. I remember one night after a particular party, I dropped all of my friends at home since I was the only one with a car and I proceeded to drive home, drunk and sleepy at 4:00am. Struggling to stay awake and stay on the road, it is only by God's grace that I am here today to share these experiences. Many times we stumble for quite some time until we reach a pivotal turning point in our lives. We must be thankful however if we come to the turning point sooner rather than later as we can sometimes make a terrible mess of our lives searching in many different places for the peace and hope that only Christ provides.

My lifestyle would continue in this cycle for about a year until one day my mother received a phone call from a priest and close friend of my grandmother, Fr. Ian Taylor. He invited us both to start a program in church called a Life in the Spirit Seminar. My mother agreed but I was not keen on doing anything that related to church or God since I was still incredibly angry with God and the circumstances that he had "caused" in my opinion. So my answer was a clear "No!" However, my mother convinced me and told me that starting this program would make my grandmother very proud. Those words broke something in me, and even though I was still incredibly reluctant to do anything related to God and church, I went knowing that this would have been something that would have pleased my beloved grandmother.

I remember walking into the church that first night at eighteen years old, the first thing that struck me was the number of young people I saw close to my age. They all seemed incredibly happy and they were all jumping, clapping and raising their hands in the air praising God. I remember being in such shock. This was something I had never seen before. The only time I saw young people enjoy themselves like that was in the clubs and parties that I would go. I looked on with a keen interest. I wondered if it was genuine, I felt like I was being pranked and they would all soon leave and the old people would come in with the organs and we would sing the hymns that put people to sleep, but I was wrong. It was real and as I would come to experience on my own, it is the most real we ever are because it is in fact what we were created to do. We will clarify this in the chapter on Perspective later on. I looked on intensely, I listened to the instruments, the rhythm, the voices, it was all so beautiful and it was all so foreign to me. I saw the joy on people's faces, I could tell it was real. I could tell it penetrated below the surface, it was something that was emanating from within. I had no idea what it was at that point, but it enthralled me.

That first night I came to understand what a Life in the Spirit seminar was. It was an eight week program which was meant to ignite and deepen one's faith in Jesus through the power of the Holy Spirit. I didn't fully understand what all these terms meant on my first night but I remember as we were split into groups, everything my group leader said about sin and living a different life started stirring up something within me and while I didn't understand everything, it sparked my interest and made me anxious to return. While driving home that night something changed, something provoked my thoughts. I wondered what did it mean to live for Christ and if it was something I could really enjoy. Soon enough though I would remember the terrible experiences that God allowed to happen to me and those inquisitive thoughts were shut out.

Week after week though, I continued to go and I continued to learn. I was introduced to this term called Salvation in a very real and potent way. I also learned other terms such as Repentance, Grace and Mercy. These were all words that were tossed around quite often having grown up in a Catholic home, but now, they bore a special type of credence for me. They started resonating personally. I remember specifically one week my group leader spoke about God allowing us to go through particular circumstances to shape and prepare us for what our future holds. I wondered to myself if, maybe I had gone through these tragic experiences to prepare me for something later on. I didn't quite know yet but I was starting to process the idea that maybe this was all part of some greater plan.

The end of the seminar would climax with the "Baptism in the Holy Spirit". I remember our group leaders telling us that we would receive different gifts of the Holy Spirit like the apostles received at Pentecost and it seemed quite overwhelming. I didn't really want to speak in "tongues" or anything of the sort. I found it all to be a bit too much but under the guidance of our leaders at the time, we trusted that whatever gifts God would give us would be for our "good". The day was finally upon us and our fears had been temporarily alleviated through the reassuring words of our leaders. I remember we were all gathered together about one hundred and twenty of us and Fr. Taylor said "Ok we will now welcome God's Holy Spirit". The moment had arrived and I had no idea what it would be like. Little did I know, it would be the single most powerful moment of my entire life.

I remembered my eyes being closed and feeling nothing. I thought to myself maybe it was all just an act of some sort. I felt a bit disappointed as if I was not good enough to experience all of the wonderful spiritual things that we were promised. Then, suddenly after a few minutes everything changed. I felt this very warm presence take over me and experienced this very bright light. To this day I cannot fully explain the feeling but every time I think about it, it is absolutely certain to me that it was not a feeling that I have experienced from anything in this world. It was a moment where I felt completely and thoroughly loved and it was a love I immediately wanted others to experience. In that moment, all the pain of losing both my grandmother and father left me in an instant and I was given an inner sense of assurance that they were now okay. I also became emotional thinking of the many times I turned my back on God and his love for me never changed, much like the story of the prodigal son. He allowed me to have my way for a while then sparked the change that was needed. The immediate change was apparent as Fr. asked if anyone would like to share their experience. Normally, I would have been a very timid person and would have dreaded the thought of speaking in front of anyone but upon hearing the question I jolted up out of my seat and stood in front of a packed church sharing my experience. The experience would allow me to realize and harness gifts I knew never existed.

Many things changed after that experience in 2010. I rediscovered a passion I had for music from an early age and was encouraged to join the music ministry. I would soon develop abilities on the guitar and keyboard and this would go on to become one of the passions dearest to my heart.

A new life had begun, one where I found joy in doing things for God. The faith moved from a one day of the week event to a lifestyle. One single moment had transformed everything. I realized I could no longer continue living the life that I was and I needed to make changes. I gave up going to certain places, removed myself from certain social circles, I remember being so passionate in those early years. Though the roots did not yet run deep, the seed was certainly planted and the soil was rich. The zeal was fresh and every time I encountered a question which I could not answer, I would spend endless time online reading and learning how to defend and explain various aspects of the faith. I knew that if what I believed about Jesus was true, then I needed to be able to explain this to others so that they too could understand the love and joy that I experienced. Sharing Christ and his teachings would eventually become a passion for me. I knew that what I experienced was real and I knew the place God brought me from and I wanted others to have the same encounter.

After some years of being exposed to various aspects of the faith and learning a tremendous amount, I was eventually asked to preach at one event. I remember thinking to myself "These people really want *me* to preach?" I was so incredibly nervous and afraid mainly because I did not view myself as worthy. I viewed preachers, pastors and priests at a certain pinnacle of holiness which I had not yet achieved and I did not feel worthy to be considered in that class of people. I have now come to realize that we are all simply vessels radiating God's love and grace in different ways.

I said 'yes' to that opportunity to preach and that turned out to be the path to countless doors that would be opened that I could have never imagined. From that small 'yes' to his will, I have been blessed with the opportunity to share my story and God's word in many different parts of the country, the Caribbean, the US and as far as Europe and I am incredibly humbled. The message here though is not about me or placing myself on any pedestals, it is about what God can do through our obedience to him. One theme always rings true wherever I go. Everyone is in need of a way out of their trials. Everyone is searching but not everyone is finding. To be able to be given the opportunity to share a message with someone that could be the most important word they could ever hear is a task that I take seriously.

I remember one particular time sharing in the US Virgin Island of St Thomas, and it was the first time I broke down in tears while speaking. The magnitude of the moment came over me. I thought of where I came from, the dark place I was and how God was using me and my former darkness to help others. Many of the people in the crowd that particular day came up to me at the end of that sharing, many of them in tears and many of them had been through similar experiences and were able to find hope through my story. It was then everything came together full circle in my mind. I realized that the tragedies that we go through provide triumphs for another and though we may not understand while in the moment, God always uses our story for a bigger purpose which we will one day understand!

We must understand though that even after coming to Christ we will still struggle, fall and suffer, in fact challenges will increase because you are now more of a threat to the enemy. There will be a difference though with how we endure the suffering if we allow God to work in and through us, we will operate through a different perspective - A victorious one.

Reflections on Suffering:

I encourage you to reflect silently on the following questions after reading the previous chapter:

- Is there any hurt, pain or situation that I find too difficult to hand over to God?

- Could there be a deeper lesson that God is trying to teach me through my current suffering?

- Am I content with where I have placed God in my life?

Affirmations:

- There is no suffering too great for God to deliver me from.

- He is always present even in my darkest moments.

- I will embrace the transformation and healing that my suffering will bring.

- His power is made perfect in my weakness.

LOVE

Love is always patient and kind; love is never jealous; love is not boastful or conceited, it is never rude and never seeks its own advantage, it does not take offence or store up grievances. Love does not rejoice at wrongdoing, but finds its joy in the truth. It is always ready to make allowances, to trust, to hope and to endure whatever comes. 1 Corinthians 13:4-7

When we experience God's love personally, something changes within us and if we let it, we start viewing situations not for what they are in themselves but for the invaluable lessons they teach us and the selfless beings we become.

Sadly, our society has oversimplified the word "Love" in many ways and it has become quite casually used in daily parlance. Our Ancient Greek counterparts have described the term in a much more granular manner, having four different words for love.

The first type of love is called **Eros.** Eros is the type of love which refers specifically to the burning passion and desire for each other in a physical sense. While this has validity in the context of marriage, it was considered to be dangerous by the Greeks since it was mostly characterized by a lack of self-control. What is even more startling is that when we observe society today, terms such as being 'madly in love' propose a similar abandonment of self-control, allowing physical desire and satisfaction to consume the essence of relationships. It is also seemingly the type of love promoted and spewed through modern day culture. The media through Hollywood, social media and mainstream television has done an excellent job of glamorizing promiscuity and reducing the value of virginity, purity and faithfulness.

The second type of love is called **Philia.** This constitutes a deep and genuine friendship for each other which the Greeks valued deeper than the carnal nature of sexuality. It represented doing good and wanting the best for another person, being open to assist one another in times of need, genuinely caring and being present in another's time of distress.

The third type of love is called **Storge.** It is commonly described as the love between family members but more specifically relates to the deep love a parent has for a child. It is natural and unforced. Broadly speaking, it is a love of unity which keeps family structures in place.

The final and highest form of love is referred to as **Agape**. This is the unconditional, radical love of another. It loves without receiving anything in return and is unchanging. It is the self-sacrificing to will the good of another. This is the remarkable display of love which Jesus showed by dying for us on the cross.

In the gospel of John 21:15-17, Jesus asks Peter "Peter, do you love me?" Jesus asked this using the Greek word *agape*, illustrating his unconditional love for Peter. Peter responds "Yes, Lord, you know I love you", however, Peter responds with the word *phileo* which is more of a brotherly love as described above. Jesus recognized this and asked him again using the same *agape* version of love and Peter yet again responds with the *phileo* version of love. It is evident that Jesus was trying to impress upon Peter the need to expand the current boundaries of his love, that which would only take place upon his receiving the Holy Spirit in Acts chapter 1.

Jesus very clearly speaks to all of us when he asks Peter this question. Insert your name when Jesus asks the question above and ask yourself how do you love Jesus? Do you love him because you were taught to? Because he has blessed you with talents and gifts? Maybe you love him because you believe it's the right thing to do? I am quite certain if we ask a congregation of churchgoers on a Sunday morning if they love Jesus their answer will be a resounding 'YES!' However if we drill deeper and ask how many would be willing to sacrifice something dear to them for Jesus, it may be quite a different answer. Love seems quite popular until it demands sacrifice but if it is unwilling to sacrifice, it is not *agape*.

The truth is we are all called to this highest level of love for both God and for each other. Unconditional love is one which wills the good of the other. If we look at Jesus' example, every action of his life was made with our good in mind. He put his feelings aside because of the decision he made to love us for our good. This is why his act of dying for us was the perfect act of love; he did it not because he had to but because he chose to. If we are honest with ourselves, how many of us would willingly suffer for the good of another? Even if we reduce the stakes, sometimes we are barely comfortable with giving another person a lift in our cars, far more for an act of love like St Maximilian Kolbe which we will discuss later on.

Sadly, what is heavily promoted in today's society is an *eros* type of love, the love which the Greeks considered to be the most basic, carnal level of love, the burning sexual desire that drives us to want one another physically. The fact is, though, when that desire fades and there comes a time where sacrifice is required, the pillars of most relationships and marriages start to crumble. It is no surprise that one out of every three marriages in the US ends in divorce. I propose that it is primarily because most of us have never been taught how to truly love in an *agape* sense.

Agape love is completely sacrificial. It shifts the question from 'what can I get out of this?' to 'how much more can I put into this for the good of another and myself?' It is always ready to give and it is much more of a decision than a feeling; a decision that despite whatever situational factors may change in our relationships, there is a commitment to do what is right and true for ourselves and for another.

We must also understand that it is not that there is something wrong with the other types of love illustrated by the Greeks. They all have some level of good in them, for example, *eros* love and desire is necessary to create that powerful physical and emotional bond between a husband and wife. *Philia* love is good in the sense that it promotes charitable acts towards each other such as giving of alms and helping those less fortunate. *Storge* love is essential for love to reign within families and for family life to be healthy and cohesive. However, *Agape* love encompasses all others and this is the standard by which we are called to love as followers of Christ.

How then are we to love in an *Agape* sense in a world which promotes self-satisfaction and immediate gratification?

The answer is the Holy Spirit. The Holy Spirit essentially gives us personal insight into the heart of God. He recreates our heart and will us unto his. He reveals this unconditional love to us and grants the perseverance required to consistently decide on willing the good of another despite the cost. It is this same spirit which Jesus promises to us in John 16:7. Jesus tells his disciples that it is better for them if he goes so that he can send his Holy Spirit to be with them. He understood quite clearly the necessity and the tremendous value of the Holy Spirit in our lives for us to live and love as he did. This is made abundantly clear in the transformation in the lives of the apostles throughout the book of Acts. Twelve men who were completely dejected and broken after the death of their brother, friend and leader experienced not merely encouragement and inspiration but a complete transformation and renewal of their hearts and minds. It is what ignited their faith and gave them the burning desire and love to preach the gospel of the resurrected Christ to the ends of the earth. This could have only been done through an *agape* love brought about by a personal encounter with Jesus through his Holy Spirit at Pentecost.

Below is an account of how each of the apostles reportedly died:

1. **Peter** - The Roman emperor Nero authorized his killing around 66 AD. Peter willingly accepted and requested to be crucified upside down because he

did not consider himself worthy to die in the same manner as his Lord.

2. **Andrew** - After reportedly taking the gospel to the Soviet Union, he ended his mission in Asia Minor (modern day Turkey) where he was crucified on an X shaped cross.

3. **Thomas** - Tradition accounts Thomas preaching to the east of Syria and as far as India. He was reportedly killed in India by the spears of four soldiers.

4. **Phillip -** After converting the wife of a proconsul in North Africa, the proconsul had him arrested and put to death. It is reported that he was pierced with hooks in his ankles and hung upside down to die in tremendous agony.

5. **Matthew-** The tax collector and author of the first of the synoptic gospels. Details on his death have been debated; some say he did not die a martyr's death while others claim he was stabbed to death in Ethiopia. Either way, he ministered the gospel in Persia and Ethiopia out of love and passion till his death.

6. **Bartholomew** - Spent much of his mission with Thomas in India and also in Ethiopia and Arabia. The most common account of his death was through whipping, tearing his flesh to shreds until he bled to death.

7. **James, son of Zebedee** - Ministered in Syria. By accounts of the historian Josephus, he was stoned and clubbed to death.

8. **James Alpheus** - We know he lived at least five years after the death of Christ because of mentions in the Bible. According to tradition, James son of Alpheus was thrown down from the temple by the Scribes and Pharisees; he was then stoned, and his brains dashed out with a fuller's club.

9. **Simon the Zealot -** Ministered in Persia and was killed after refusing to sacrifice to the sun god.

10. **Matthias** - The apostle chosen to replace Judas, accompanied Andrew to Syria and was reportedly burned to death.

11. **Jude -** Was crucified after doing missionary work in Persia.

12. **John -** The youngest of the Apostles and Jesus' beloved, was the only one who reportedly died naturally of old age on the Greek island of Patmos.

13. **Judas Iscariot -** Shortly after the death of Christ, Judas killed himself. According to the Bible he hanged himself (Matthew 27:5) at Aceldama, on the southern slope of the valley of Hinnom, near Jerusalem, and in the act he fell down a precipice and was dashed into pieces.

14. **Paul** - Not one of the twelve but still an apostle in his own regard, was beheaded in Rome.

The consistent theme above with the exception of Judas is love through suffering. There is no love without suffering. One would expect that in the face of severe persecution, at least some of the apostles would renounce their belief but this is precisely what *agape* love represents. It is a decision to love and will the good of others despite the cost. Each of them represented this up to the end of their lives because they emulated the one who did it perfectly. Moreover, they understood that what they believed was irrevocably true. Many of them left families, households and an entire way of Jewish life to embrace this call. It is easy for us to miss the significance of this through our contemporary lens.

The Jews had strict commandments that they believed wholeheartedly were from God, many of which were punishable by death if they were broken because they considered death to be the fitting punishment for offending God. Consider what it would have taken for first century Jews to STOP adhering to their ancient laws such as circumcision or keeping the Sabbath holy. Something extraordinary would have had to take place for them to risk not just becoming socially outcast but to also offend God, the most grievous offense in their eyes. Something absolutely life changing had to occur, something transformative, something that would impress upon them that Jesus was sent by God the Father himself and was the Messiah for whom they waited centuries. Something like….a resurrection.

They had to know and believe wholeheartedly that what they had been taught was fulfilled in the person of Jesus Christ and the only reasonable explanation for this is that they were first hand eye witnesses to his death out of love but more importantly the same man whose death was witnessed was also seen alive in the flesh by all of them.

Paul accounts in his first letter to the Corinthians Chapter 15 that Jesus appeared to more than 500 persons after his death and also goes onto to say that the entire essence of the Christian gospel is hinged on the resurrection being not just a concept but an actual historical event that took place. Paul understood this and wrote at a time where if untrue, many of his contemporaries would have condemned his claims. Instead they were reinforced by the persons of his time and the gospel writers because they all experienced the risen Christ physically. It is this same risen Christ we all experience spiritually today, 2000 years later through the power of his Holy Spirit and physically through the Eucharist.

Let us return to the crucifixion and agape love, for a second. We know the apostles showed elements of agape love by the way they lived and died but the perfect act of agape love shown was when Jesus uttered the words "Father, forgive them for they know not what they do". Jesus certainly could have easily switched the narrative and the crucifixion scene could have ended quite differently in a fit of anger and revenge. However, he illustrated the perfect act of love by asking his father to forgive the very individuals responsible for his torture and death. This is the example which each of the apostles followed under the anointing of the Holy Spirit. We must understand that this standard was not simply set for the apostles but for all humanity. The apostles were no different from us. They are not to be placed on a throne of holiness as they were all sinners just like you and I. What they did have, however, was insight into their own fragile nature and complete openness to the spirit of God. That openness led to conviction, conversion and to the personification of *agape* love poured out into their hearts by the Holy Spirit. This is not impossible.

We can sometimes become overwhelmed with the seemingly daunting task of living a holy life or telling another person about Jesus, overlooking the fact that a holy life is simply a collection of holy moments. But what in fact is a holy moment? It is a moment where we listen to and obey the will of God for our life. However, we can only know his will if we know his voice and we can only know his voice if we isolate ourselves from the noise of life every now and then to listen. John 10:27 tells us "My sheep hear my voice, and I know them, and they follow me." If we are his sheep, we know his voice and his expectation of us. We must actively seek out the time to learn the voice of the shepherd.

None of us knows what tomorrow holds, nor what next week, month or the next ten or twenty years may hold but we do have right now and we can choose him right now. You may claim to be unworthy but think for a second of how Paul felt in Romans chapter 7. He lamented on how he struggled with personal sin and that every time he tried to do the right thing he failed and did the wrong. We can all find ourselves in Paul. Ironically, if you live in the Western part of the world, it is Paul you have to thank for your knowledge of Jesus today as he was responsible for spreading the faith to the non-Jewish world; he also wrote just about half of the New Testament. The same Paul who felt unworthy, struggled with personal sin and also authorized the murder of those who believed in Jesus.

If Jesus could show his love to Paul, transform him, teach him how to love and fill his heart with the boldness and courage to persevere amidst persecution until the end, how much more will he use you? Think of the circumstances I highlighted in my own life earlier. I had no idea that the teenage boy who lost his dad at sixteen and grandmother at seventeen and spiraled into fornication and promiscuity would be the same person who would share those same experiences in front of hundreds of people one day around the world and bring conviction and conversion. I still remain in awe sometimes, but it reminds me all the more that God is good and this journey is not about me but it's about him – knowing him and leading others to do the same.

We each have a purpose in God, one that leads to salvation for yourself and others with whom you will come into contact. Blessed are those who are brave and open enough to discover this purpose. Perhaps it will come to you as you read these pages, maybe it will come next week, or in a few years, but the sooner, the better as we all have a role to play in this grand story of bridging the gap from earth to eternity through the *agape* love of Christ.

No one can have greater love than to lay down his life for his friends. John 15:12

A perfect example of a man who lived the very words of this scripture to his death, other than Jesus himself, was St. Maximilian Kolbe. Born Raymond Kolbe on January 8th 1894, Raymond was deeply grieved by the political climate in Poland as a child and dreamed of political reunification. He had a special affinity to the Blessed Virgin Mary and would often plead her intercession fervently from an early age. A pivotal moment in Raymond's life occurred one day when he was naturally being a mischievous little boy. His mother reprimanded him and asked him what would become of him if his naughty behavior continued. Sorrowfully Raymond asked the same question of the Blessed Virgin Mary.

She showed him a vision of two crowns: one red, the other white. When asked to choose which he preferred, he chose both: to remain pure and undivided in his love for God and the Blessed Virgin, and to be a martyr. It is clear from a very early age, Raymond Kolbe knew clearly the call placed upon his heart and was determined to live out that call.

He would become famously known for his act of perfect selflessness and love when his beloved country of Poland became the victim of Nazi death camps in 1941. When one of the prisoners escaped, Nazi officers decided to put ten men to death as punishment for this escape. One of these men happened to be a husband and father who felt deep agony at the thought of never seeing his wife and children again. Raymond, now Fr. Maximilian Kolbe, saw the agony faced by the prisoner and decided to offer his own life in his place. The guards willingly obliged and Maximilian was sentenced to death by starvation.

Devoid of food or water for two weeks, Maximilian should have already been dead but instead he led other prisoners in praying the rosary and other prayers. Guards realizing that he was still alive eventually issued him a lethal injection which ultimately killed him. The level of sacrifice and unwavering faith which was shown by Maximilian resulted in him being declared a Saint by the Church through Pope Saint John Paul II on October 10, 1982.

The prologue highlights our call to sainthood, it does not necessarily mean that we are all called to give up our lives for another but one thing is certain, we do not inherit eternity without being fully open to the path which God has called us. Love, however, makes the difference. When we come to understand the unconditional love God has for us, only then can we be fully at peace with listening to his voice in our lives and responding out of love in return to wherever that voice may lead us.

Reflections on Love:

- Is my love for God dependent on his answering my prayers?

- Can I say I love God when bad things happen to me?

- Do I continue to love him when I do not feel his presence?

- How confident am I that others see the love of Christ in me?

- Do I recognize Jesus' death for me as the perfect act of love?

Affirmations

- God has loved me and will always love me all the days of my life.

- We show our love for God through our love for each other.

- I am called to love unconditionally and sacrificially because I am loved unconditionally and sacrificially.

IDENTITY

The concept of our identity continues to be an Achilles' heel for many Christians. Even though God's word is littered with examples of broken men and women who have received new life in Christ, we are continually plagued with feelings of unworthiness and still become bogged down with the opinions and considerations of others. Let's face it, how someone feels about us matters to us, even when we pretend it is not so. Many may try to show stoic indifference, at least externally, when an unpopular opinion is expressed to them but for most, opinions matter and for a particularly large number, they matter deeply, but how deeply should opinions affect us as believers in Christ?

This brings about the question of our identity and to whom we are called. Jeremiah 1:5 tells us "Before I formed you in the womb I knew you, before you were born, I consecrated you." We are all consecrated for God's work. Consecrate comes from the Latin word *consecrare* which originally meant to make sacred or holy, which means that from the beginning, God set us apart for his very particular plan of holiness and it is in this our identity lies. However, if we spend most of our time engulfed in the opinions of others, we can find ourselves fitting into the boxes others place us in.

The word 'holiness' itself can be a bit intimidating for some and also perceived as boring for others but we need to be careful of what we perceive holiness to be. It does not always fit the traditional view of pious, clasped hands or being prostrated in adoration or silent prayer. As stated previously in the chapter on love, holiness is a life of consistent virtue. This can range from being obedient and doing chores, to listening to someone in their time of trouble or even sharing a meal with someone. Holiness looks different to many because God moves in us differently and prompts us to act in different ways, which may not always be easily understood by peers. God may convict you of a particular aspect of your life that he has not yet convicted another person of and their inability to understand that can often come across as judgement or classing someone in a condescending light.

I remember just starting off my walk of faith, freshly baptized in the Holy Spirit at age nineteen and ready to evangelize. I was still a student at the University of the West Indies (UWI) and many of my friends reminded me of the 'old me'. They still saw the Jameke who partied, smoked and got drunk and it made me even start to question my own identity. I started believing that maybe I was the same person. Maybe this church 'thing' was not for me and it became a battle for me. One of the first things I had to recognize along the journey was that it was not simply a 'church thing' but a conscious decision I had made to pursue a deeper relationship with God and that this decision would now be the corner stone from which other decisions would flow. I would soon realize that pursuing a relationship with God was not simply a label that is worn that erases all of life's problems rather it is actively reminding myself of who I am in God's eyes through prayer, his word and the teachings of the church and that this would now be a lifelong exercise. Looking back now, I believe it is a failure of most of us within active ministry. We may bring people to an encounter with Jesus but after that we leave them to figure out the rest of their life on their own and many often fall back into previous sinful habits. After the encounter, we require deep formation and support. We may even need someone to walk with us and guide us along the way because though we are transformed through the power of God's Holy Spirit, we still battle with our sinful nature and the voices and opinions of others. Those who may have gone through this and have overcome it should be there to provide support and guidance to new believers just as Paul did through his letters to the new churches he established.

Though sin may be forgiven when we come to Christ, the desire to sin is etched deeply within us and it is not something we can glibly deny. Christians who claim perfection are truly the furthest from Christ, because Paul himself after his transformation said we are called to avidly *work out* our salvation with fear and trembling. We must be prepared daily to fight the battle for our souls, welcome things that will help the fight and shut out those which will lead to our demise. So what does all of this have to do with our identity and who we are in God's eyes?

Human beings are generally apt at pointing out each other's shortcomings but we ought to be wary of the opinions we allow to give us validation. Let us examine a few who rose above the opinions of others as it relates to us and our own journey.

David was the smallest and least physically commanding of all of his brothers, yet it was he who God chose to become King over the Israelite people, subsequently slaying the giant Goliath. Everyone including David's own family doubted him and his ability but God chose him. David would go on to become one of the most powerful kings of Israel and write most of the psalms of the Bible. The Lord also highlighted quite clearly in 1 Samuel 16:7 "Do not consider his appearance or his height, for I have rejected him. The Lord does not look at the things people look at. People look at the outward appearance, but the Lord looks at the heart." It illustrates quite clearly that God does not view us in the same way that we view each other. While we have opinions on who we think may be the most capable, strong, talented or even holy, God sees quite clearly the condition of our hearts and knows our truest potential since he made us. He is not concerned with apparent physical or intellectual advantages and limitations. We must never forget that if he has called us, he will empower us to do that which we are called and therein lies our validation and identification.

The first step in understanding our identity then should be in realizing that we are made in the image and likeness of God himself and thus designed to live eternally in communion with him. Secondly, we are loved unconditionally and there is no sin that changes the degree of that love. Our walk as Christians should then be characterized with the primary emphasis that we are beings created out of love, for love and to love.

Saul was a devout Jew and an avid persecutor of the Christian faith and even authorizing the killing of several Christians, until he was blinded by Jesus himself on the road to Damascus. This encounter subsequently transformed him into Paul the dynamic apostle. Despite his transformation, many still sought his death because he was now a traitor to his previous identity. Paul resolved to embrace the fact that he was now a new creation in Christ and would go on to find his purpose serving the one true living God spreading his name to the ends of the earth. This should open our eyes. God has a specific way in which he has planned to use us with our cooperation. He will not force his will upon us, but he will provide subtle or sometimes blatant signs as to the course we should chart in this life. Imagine the tremendous gift we could be robbing the world of by not listening to the call that God has placed on our hearts and choosing to listen to the opinions of others who may not have our best interest at heart.

We can also think of ourselves as instruments. Instruments are designed to produce wonderful sounds by those with the ability to play. Conversely, if they are used by those with no knowledge of playing, we wind up with useless noise. Sadly this is what many of us do when we allow others to give us validity with toxic opinions. We give those who are ill-equipped to play our instrument an opportunity to play and many times, the result is a useless life. However, when we allow ourselves to be fully used by God then we allow ourselves to be utilized by the one who is perfectly equipped to do so since he designed us. It is then we truly come to understand who we are as children of God and why our identity is critical to living an empowered daily Christian life, then the music of our lives becomes quite beautiful indeed!

If we understand the above scripture in totality in conjunction with the examples above, we should understand that God cleans the slate when we embrace his call upon our lives. Though others may continually remind us of our pasts, God does not and this is the crux of the matter. This is then, where we place opinions on who we are in the grand scheme of things. Christ has defined us and will judge us upon death, so he is the person we should be exerting the greatest energy and effort in trying to please.

It is incredibly easy to get lost in pleasing others, ensuring that we're politically and socially correct, at the expense of who God has called us to be. In the end, we will stand before God alone. We will be called to give an account of our lives and our shortcomings and, unfortunately, not serving him because of how others view us will be an invalid excuse when it's all said and done. He has given us enough examples - countless men and women who have persevered in faith till the very end who allowed themselves to be identified by the one who created them.

It's similar to a parent preparing a child to defend against bullies at school. Parents reinforce the child's mind with positive statements like "You are beautiful", "You are intelligent", "I love you". These are not simply platitudes to make the child feel good. The parent speaks these truths because the parent knows the child better than anyone else. When the child is then faced with slurs from bullies such as "You are stupid" and "You are ugly" the child is better equipped to respond to these attacks because their identity has already been reinforced by their parents. Bullies would then stand a much lower chance of destroying the child's self-esteem. It's the same with God, us and the opinions of others. If we let the opinions of others constantly define, hurt and shape us, it is primarily because we have not sufficiently reinforced who we are in God's eyes. God's word is there to provide the greatest form of encouragement, support, advice and help that we need so let his words, the words of our heavenly father, identify us instead of the voices of the world. Reinforce your identity with his word!

Mother Teresa captures these thoughts quite aptly in one of her most famously attributed quotes:

"People are often unreasonable, irrational, and self-centered. Forgive them anyway.
If you are kind, people may accuse you of selfish, ulterior motives. Be kind anyway.
If you are successful, you will win some unfaithful friends and some genuine enemies.
Succeed anyway.
If you are honest and sincere people may deceive you. Be honest and sincere anyway.
What you spend years creating, others could destroy overnight. Create anyway.
If you find serenity and happiness, some may be jealous. Be happy anyway.
The good you do today, will often be forgotten. Do good anyway.
Give the best you have, and it will never be enough. Give your best anyway.
In the final analysis, it is between you and God.

It was never between you and them anyway."

I believe it is one of the most accurate representations of the ultimate and most important relationship that we ought to spend our time cultivating - that between us and God. We make these types of discussions so rare and taboo in today's society that speaking of it almost makes one seem delusional and outcasts most from regular daily conversations. It is precisely this type of thinking that perpetuates the notion that sainthood is such an unattainable feat, only reserved for the selected few. If we would only realize the brokenness and humanity of the saints we would realize that it is a title to which we should all ascribe because it is a title of humility as opposed to one of grandeur and superiority. Often, one has to be brought to the lowest places to fully realize their identity in Christ and it is in these low places we recognize our desperate need for God's intervention.

Mother Teresa understood clearly the perspective required. She spent most of her life serving in the poorest of places in India not because she sought any glory or recognition, but because she found her call and identity in Christ and lived out that call to fruition.

I do not wish for the words in this book to sound like an idealistic or euphoric reality; rather, I would like us all to realize that sainthood is the call upon each of our lives and it is attainable. The decision is ours to continuously say "No" to sin and "Yes" to God. How we will all achieve that is up to us as we all have different journeys but we must escape the routine of constantly selling ourselves short because we make time for everything else in our lives except that to which God has called us.

There has to be an eternal focus on him in our daily lives for us to experience the fullness of life which exists in him. We sometimes feel the need to reduce the words of Jesus for fear of sounding too radical or over spiritual while the world vehemently pushes sinful agendas without any reservations as to whom it may offend. For me, it has been a beautiful thing to experience a freedom and joy that no one can take away in the midst of the mundane rigor and fluctuations of life. He continues to be my constant and I believe if my identity is found in something constant, then it remains unwavering despite others' opinions. It also creates a tremendous level of responsibility knowing that our actions and decisions here on earth bear eternal weight. We discussed fleeting desires in an earlier chapter, it is quite clear yet again that human opinions fall into this category. We cannot allow ourselves to be continuously defined by the ever-changing nature of human opinions as we will not please everyone. For us to live a life with foundation, the essence of who we are must be rooted in the one who is unchanging.

Footnote

For clarification purposes, I am not prescribing here that we completely abandon others' opinions as God may also place people in your life to provide correction, advice and positive critiques but we need to discern through the Holy Spirit. To put it simply, God will not send someone into our lives to give advice or assistance with a message that is contradictory to his word. This is the clear standard and lens through which we identify ourselves and our purpose. Discern well!

Reflections on Identity

- Am I defining myself by my shortcomings?

- How important are others' opinions to me?

- Am I allowing myself to be defined by others' opinions?

- Am I feeling unworthy of God's love?

Affirmations

- I am not defined by my past or my sins, but by God's love for me.

- I am not defined by the opinions of others

- I am a new creation in Christ, old things have passed away.

- If God has called me, he will empower me to do that which he has called.

- I will actively spend silent time with God discovering his will for me.

- I will live in his purpose for my life, as difficult as that may be.

PERSPECTIVE

Our hearts are restless until they rest in you ~ St Augustine of Hippo 'Confessions Book 1, Chapter 1'

Christianity in essence is the poignant realization that the soul is displaced in its current position and requires a transformation through grace for it to be restored to its eternal communion in God. As St. Augustine points out, the soul is restless without God. Unsettled at best. There are many beautiful moments to be experienced in this life. Completing one's university degree, marrying one's true love, witnessing the birth of a firstborn, an uplifting conversation, laughter with a friend, obtaining a long awaited promotion, obtaining financial freedom, purchasing one's home, quality time with good friends. All of these give us some sort of satisfaction and can determine relevance in our lives in some way, even providing some sort of worth or identity. However, so many of us do all of the above and still feel incomplete as if there were something more to be gained, something beyond the physical. This is a desire etched within each of us whether we realize it or not.

I recall one point in my life when I was eighteen years old, I had recently started university and inherited my grandmother's car. The most important thing for me then was purchasing a set of brand new chrome rims for my car. Trivial as it may sound, it meant a lot to me and all of my spending and saving patterns were designed with this as the goal. I saved for months; some days I wouldn't even buy lunch just to put aside a little extra to have my car fitted with those rims. The thought pervaded my mind. I couldn't wait for the day when I would purchase it and take pictures. Silly as this sounds now, we are all very similar as human beings. For me at eighteen years old it was rims. For you at twenty eight it may be your wedding day. For another at forty eight, it may be their children's success in examinations. The day finally arrived and I made the purchase. I was incredibly elated, but as the days passed I realized something that many of us may already have. Much of my enjoyment and splendor came from the anticipation of the 'thing' rather than the 'thing' itself. Now that I had the rims, there was nothing else to look forward to. Each day that would pass, it would look less and less attractive. Some days it became incredibly dirty, I did not even have a desire to clean it. I soon realized that this diminishing utility that I started to experience pervades all of our lives. We pride ourselves with novelty, but because we are beings created with desires beyond the senses, we find ourselves with the pertinent question of 'Now what?'

I recall a similar example of a colleague of mine; he told me he could not wait for the day he got married and was finally intimate with his wife. Months before the wedding, I recall his anticipation and how excited he had become knowing that they both waited and that they were now going to do this great act. Since he was my good friend, I shared in his joy and commended him on doing the right thing. However, there was something slightly misplaced with his expectations. He looked forward to the physical intimacy as the defining factor of the marriage. Even though they were both chaste and prided themselves on doing the right thing, they saw the right thing as an end in itself, an act which would bring them both the greatest satisfaction needed. Soon after, we had many conversations relating to married life where he confessed that although sex was a beautiful act, he had put too much of his hope in it, in fact, all of his hope. After two years of marriage, he has since had to find other things to build, sustain and maintain a more holistic and deeper bond between them. Thankfully they have been successful thus far and have managed to still have a healthy marriage.

The point here is that nothing ultimately satisfies except Christ. It is all transitory - money, sex, wealth, power. Christian apologist Ravi Zacharias says "Skeptics say it is the problem of pain that keeps them from believing in God, may I suggest to you it is the problem of pleasure that keeps me from being a skeptic." It is quite clear to see within our own selves, etched deep within us there is a longing for more. Sex, money, and power - none of it fills the void and the skeptic has yet to provide any way to satisfy the deeper longing that exists in man. The wealthy and powerful are often the most miserable. Comedian and actor Jim Carrey who has a net worth of 150 million USD is quoted as saying "I think everybody should get rich and famous and do everything they ever dreamed of so they can see that it's not the answer." NBA Athlete Demar DeRozan who has a net worth of 139 million USD and continuously battles depression echoed similar words saying "...I wish everyone in the world was rich so they would realize that money isn't everything." Multimillionaires have access to essentially any material thing at their fingertips and they still yearn for more. Many of them develop drug addictions, some even reach the point of suicide. Why? Pleasure seeking does not provide a meaningful life, it in fact provides quite the opposite as many would attest. The emptiest of feelings often occurs after doing or achieving that which you thought would give you the greatest satisfaction and realizing that it didn't. I am not prescribing that we strive to remain poor or intentionally suffer, however, I am clearly saying that wealth nor anything else found here will ever satisfy the deeper longing within mankind for a meaningful existence. Recently renowned Canadian clinical psychologist Jordan Peterson proposes that we find meaning in life through the responsibilities that we bear and I would like to agree with this presupposition. However, I would like to push the envelope a bit further and add that our responsibilities must first be hinged on an understanding of our identity and purpose in Jesus for the truest of meanings to be found.

Consider the following analogy: let's say Jack's grandmother purchases the IPhone X. After fiddling around with it for some time, she discovers how to make a phone call. Yet she has no idea what is Wi-Fi, no clue what mobile data means and no understanding of what is an 'App' so she asks her tech savvy fifteen year old grandson Jack to show her. Of course he whizzes through the phone's software and shows the grandmother what to do and after some time, she slowly catches on and gains some understanding. She still wants to learn more so she decides to go to the Apple Store and ask the store's attendant. The attendant calmly and willingly sits with her and thoroughly explains every single feature the phone contains and how to use it as well as some helpful shortcuts. The grandmother is amazed at just how powerful the phone is and is completely blown away by all that she has learned. Just like the grandmother above, we are looking for a way to understand ourselves, to find meaning and navigate through life and we look for help from different persons: self-help gurus, psychologists, entrepreneurs, pastors, priests, all of whom may give excellent advice but they may never fully understand our situation because they do not fully experience what we do. Although Jack helped, his grandmother only understood every single aspect of the phone when she went to the designer of the phone. More importantly, she also only then understood the power it contained and it is infinitely the same with us! There is a limit to the depth with which human words can penetrate but in order for us to find the most complete understanding of who we are, why we are here and what we are capable of, we need to go to the one who designed us! No one else will ever fully suffice.

The design of life itself points to something greater. If we follow every achievement in our lives to its logical conclusion, the 'now what?' becomes quite evident. We go to school and successfully complete a degree...now what? We go to several job interviews until we get the one we really want....now what? We work hard until we get that long awaited promotion....now what? We look for the seemingly perfect significant other and get married....now what? We save for the dream home and purchase it....now what? We have children and take care of them for several years....now what? We age and health starts to fail....now what? We finally take our last breath.....now what?! The longing for more is there because THERE IS MORE! The atheist himself usually starts with the precursor "If there was a God....." because the longing for him is there also. In a sense they would like to believe there is one as well, only under the condition of physical evidence. For millions of others, personal encounters require no evidence because the presence of God has been experienced in a powerful and tangible way.

Life is littered with many moments of personal satisfaction, but to a large extent, it's all anticipation, novelty and a cycle of fleeting desires and God is completely aware of this design. In a sense, I believe he created us with this longing so that we would search until we found him, as a being with no deeper longing would have no need for God. Certainly there are variations to the above example but the more interactions I have with people, regardless of the country, it is evident that the quest for meaning in this life is ubiquitous. This is why Jesus tells us in John 10:10 that he has come so that we may have life more abundantly. The saints understood this quite clearly and it is the reason they remained steadfast to the end. They rose above transience and found permanence in the only one who is permanent and consistent.

They understood that only Jesus enters the deep recesses of emptiness in our souls and provides us with fullness of life and purpose. It is actually something quite difficult for me to articulate since it has to be experienced through his Holy Spirit. As expressed previously, I bear testimony to the fact that I once lived a life of fleeting desires, hopping from one situation to the next, even one person to the next, to fill the void that only God could. When I did finally allow him in, it became infinitely clear that this was the single missing piece to the puzzle - a place of joy and peace in the midst of the darkest of trials. He is the calm within the storm. He is the person that speaks words of comfort into your heart when there is only chaos and tragedy. He is the one who allows you to see light within a world marred by darkness and evil and allows us to shift the perspective.

Pascal's Wager

Pascal's Wager is a proposal made by the French mathematician Blaise Pascal in the 17th century. Pascal proposed that it was reasonable to live as if God existed since there was much at stake if he did exist and nothing to lose if he did not. Some have attempted to debunk the wager over the years illustrating that it does not propose evidence that God exists, however this is not the intention here. It merely proposes that it is reasonable to live as if he did. For the sake of the writings in this book, we will examine the wager as it relates to Christianity. Let us look at what is gained if we live by the tenets of Christianity. For this, we will examine the four cardinal virtues.

Virtue by definition, is the habit or firm disposition which inclines a person to do good and avoid evil. The word 'cardinal' is derived from the Latin word 'cardo' meaning hinge; as such these four virtues are the ones from which all others are hinged. The Christian who lives and takes his faith seriously will find the active practice of doing right and all of the moral benefits of such below:

1. **<u>Prudence</u>** – Prudence is the virtue that disposes practical reason to discern our true good in every circumstance and to choose the right means of achieving it. (CCC 1806)

It is the ability to analyze a particular situation and make a proper moral judgment based on the wisdom of God regardless of the difficulty or emotion involved. The prudent person ultimately considers the benefit and consequence of one's actions and words from an eternal perspective before a decision is made. It is also referred to as 'right reason in action' as it is the virtue which lays the foundation for all Christian decision making.

An example of prudence is taking the word of God and actively applying it to daily life. For example John 13:34-35 states "Love one another as I have loved you". The prudent person will spend time asking oneself how can this word be put into practice and may ask the following question "What can I do differently today to show love to the most difficult people in my life?" We gain then, from prudence, the ability to discern, stand with integrity and act in a manner that is moral and true in the face of contrary pressure to do otherwise.

2. <u>Justice</u> - St Thomas Aquinas defines justice as "a habit whereby a man renders to each one his due with constant and perpetual will." Justice is two-fold. We are called to perform just actions toward God and secondly to our neighbour. Justice towards God involves giving him his due; this involves actively spending time in prayer, worship and obedience to his words, understanding that through them come the fullness of life. The second aspect of justice refers to how we treat each other. We are not simply called to not do wrong towards our neighbors but we are called to actively do good for each other and ensure fair and equitable treatment among all, a society where corruption ceases

to exist and we all strive towards a common good for all. It would be a gross exaggeration on my part to say that all Christians live like this, however I am stating that it is an incredibly admirable and beneficial standard to which we should aspire. GK Chesterton once said "It is not that the Christian ideal has not been tried and found wanting. It has been found difficult and left untried." Many have generalized Christianity as a set of rules and religious dogmas, but it is those who have been courageous enough to ascribe to the standard whose lives have been a tremendous source of inspiration and encouragement to the rest of the flock. Think of those who have left an indelible mark in the faith and on the world. It is not those who found the faith too difficult to follow but those who followed wholeheartedly, not blindly but believing fully in the words of Jesus to the very end. Be the few. Be remembered for your faith.

3. <u>**Fortitude**</u> - The virtue of fortitude enables a person to stand with firm resolve against the many trials and hardships of life and to remain steadfast in the pursuit of what is good. Fortitude is a quality that is needed in many areas of life as there will always be a particular circumstance that will set us back or completely derail our plans. Fortitude teaches us perseverance for that which we believe. I will even go further to say that no virtue can be achieved without some degree of fortitude, since it is necessary to withstand the many difficult temptations of this life. In the earlier part of this book, a few saints were mentioned who gave their lives for the faith. It must be noted that fortitude does not suggest the devaluing of our human lives or that it must be given or wasted frivolously in various situations, it

does, however, promote the courage to stand for what is right until the very end despite the cost.

4. <u>**Temperance**</u> - Temperance is the moral virtue that moderates the attraction of pleasures and provides balance in the use of created goods. (CCC 1808) It involves restraining passions and desires until the appointed time. It is surely not difficult to think of the consequences of a lack of temperance. Unwanted pregnancies, sickness and disease, income inequality, poverty & corruption are all a consequence of a lack of temperance and self-control. The world and more specifically western media, through the influence of Hollywood and multimillion dollar US corporations, have promoted a culture of living to satisfy immediate passions with little emphasis on the consequences of such lifestyles. Temperance in action produces self-preservation whereas the contrary vice of intemperance or self-indulgence results in self-destruction and self-degradation. John Perkins, a former "Economic Hitman", has confessed that he has worked for corporations which have gone into countries, lured them into loans which they would not have the ability to repay, under the guise of promoting economic development in the particular country. When the countries eventually default on their loans as anticipated, the corporations seize from the country whatever resources they need. Greed and manipulation at its best.

Let us consider for a second the benefits if the world were to exhibit more temperance and selflessness. Approximately 820 million people worldwide suffer from hunger. The UN estimates that it would take 30 billion dollars a year to eradicate world hunger. To put this into perspective, the US Congress budgets approximately 737 billion annually on defense. The fact that 4% of one country's defense budget is enough to end hunger worldwide is a clear indicator to me of how greed, power, and a lack of temperance has led us to the dismal realities we face today.

There are, of course, an abundance of other fruits that spring up out of the Christian faith such as love, joy, peace, patience, kindness and others, but for the sake of initial thought provocation the four cardinal virtues were mentioned to show that there are worthwhile benefits to the world and society by taking upon the 'apparent risk' of Christianity.

'In all truth I tell you, anyone who does not enter the sheepfold through the gate, but climbs in some other way, is a thief and a bandit. He who enters through the gate is the shepherd of the flock; the gatekeeper lets him in, the sheep hear his voice, one by one he calls his own sheep and leads them out. When he has brought out all those that are his, he goes ahead of them, and the sheep follow because they know his voice. They will never follow a stranger, but will run away from him because they do not recognize the voice of strangers.' John 10:1-5

There is quite a significant reference made when Jesus refers to us as sheep and himself as the shepherd. To appreciate the comparison we must understand the relationship between shepherds and sheep. Shepherds tend to hundreds of sheep and the shepherd would usually have a very specific call to which all of the sheep respond. Regardless of the many other voices or noises that the sheep hears, they only listen to and follow the voice of the shepherd. Many times, when flocks of sheep cross paths, hundreds of sheep may become intertwined with each other, however they continue to listen to the voice of their shepherd and follow him, and none are lost or left behind.

The analogy is quite relevant in our daily lives. Many of us are lost and left behind not because our shepherd isn't calling but because we are not listening. We devote our attention to the wrong things and the wrong voices. I have often heard elderly people say that one of the biggest regrets of their lives was spending too much time on things that didn't matter. For us it should go even deeper - we should be even more concerned about the things which we devote our time to because eternity is dependent on every action and decision we make in this life.

Every day we have so many different voices competing for our attention. Many of us follow other voices because they are louder, more popular or pleasing to hear. We must however, hone in on the voice of Christ in our life. This must be the voice that we follow. It is a voice that must resonate within our heart and burn within our soul in the midst of the infinite distractions that this life has to offer. He highlights that he is our good shepherd and the gate to eternal life. If this is true, we owe it to ourselves to silence all of the other voices in our lives and amplify the voice of the one who really matters - the voice of Christ, the only gate out of this degenerating world.

Here I would like to recommend the Catholic practice of Eucharistic Adoration. For Catholics who believe that Jesus is truly present in the Eucharist, this is a time spent, adoring, praising, interceding, pleading but also listening. There is no safer space to be in than the space of Jesus! It is a time of vulnerability before God allowing him to enter the very personal and intimate areas of our heart for healing, deliverance and answers. It is a space where we can completely silence the noise of our daily life and find peace in the voice of God.

Then he returned to his disciples and found them sleeping. "Simon," he said to Peter, "are you asleep? Couldn't you keep watch for one hour? Mark 14:37

I believe we can understand this text both literally and symbolically. It is literal in the sense that the disciples physically fell asleep when Jesus expected them to spend some time in prayer with him especially upon his impending arrest and torture. As highlighted in the previous scripture, Jesus was already undergoing some of the most extreme emotional torture one can endure and his plea to his apostles shows his human nature, encouraging them to ardently pray to the Father above to be able to endure the tests they were about to face.

A paradox may arise in your mind here when words such as 'emotional torture' are used to describe Jesus who is divine, omnipotent and the creator of the universe. However, we must understand the state that Jesus placed himself in while on earth. Philippians 2:7 helps us understand this concept. It tells us that he emptied himself of his divinity while here on earth, taking up the form of a servant so that he may be as we are. Jesus did not cease being God while on earth. It would appear that to illustrate Jesus' perfect humility, the manifestation of his divine power was temporarily suspended so that his humanity may have been fully relatable to those around him. It would have been no use claiming to understand our pain if by the snapping of his fingers all pain ceased in every situation. This would be the work of a genie, not a God who is relatable and personable. If we think about how we respond to others who claim to understand some tragedy in our lives, most times we respond either verbally or introspectively with the words "You have not experienced what I have". To illustrate perfectly that Jesus fully understood our pain, he had to show that he experienced our pain.

Returning to our initial point, the scripture is also metaphorical when we look at the world today. How many of us are 'sleeping' in a figurative sense? How much more tragic will it be at the end if we realized we have missed the point of everything we've experienced because we slept through the most important examination we'll ever write. If we appreciate the message for what it's worth, the symbolism is profound because the world and the enemy have pulled the wool over our eyes. We seek comfort when Jesus requests sacrifice; we seek unadulterated pleasure, when he provides self-control; we seek rest when there is tremendous work to be done for the kingdom. At some point we must evaluate if we are cognizant of what Jesus expects of us or are we caught in the post-modernist rat race of working, striving for power, pleasure seeking and dying?

It has been stated before that many rich people speak of an emptiness inside even while having the power to buy anything that can satisfy our pleasures here. The overarching message here is that we may spend our entire lives chasing what is ultimately elusive when what we needed was right in front of us all along. Do we see the free gift of salvation in front of us that Jesus is offering or are we asleep like Peter, James and John in the garden?

Do not be conformed to the pattern of this world, but be transformed by the renewing of your mind. Romans 12:2

This is a popular word, often quoted but rarely lived, when we look at the world today. It has been at the core of much contention even among believers. I believe the main issue is in the difficulty in accepting and living such a word. If we analyze the word, Paul is calling us not to mirror the sinful behavior which plagues the world but rather to renew our minds so that there is focus not just on being different from the world but a focus towards doing good in a world that is largely indifferent towards sin and evil.

The problem with this word is that the world is currently filled with many ills which at face value seem very enticing. We are constantly fed images, videos and sounds of things that we should strive for that are not necessarily godly or righteous but worldly. One may ask the question though, how do we exist in a world and not be a part of the things in the world? I will start by saying that I do not believe we are called to condemn *all* the things of the world for there are many aspects of the world that can be used for building the kingdom of God. The problem arises when we use the aspects of the world to give ourselves or the enemy glory and because this is more the norm than the alternative, trying to go against the tide can seem overwhelming. We live in a world that has become increasingly secular and selfish. The mantra of 'If it feels good, do it" seems far more appealing than "If anyone wants to be a follower of mine, let him deny himself, take up his cross daily and follow me" Luke 9:23. If, however we are called to be followers of Jesus we are called not simply to follow the word that is popular, but to follow the word that is true. Very often this means living contrary to the masses.

The question then arises as to why? Does serving God really mean I cannot party? I cannot have sex outside of marriage? I cannot have more than one wife? Why is God so overtly concerned with what I do with my personal life?

Understanding the answers to these questions comes firstly with understanding in a deeper way the reason for our existence. If it were merely to satisfy the flesh then quite certainly, it is a pitiable existence indeed. For while we all have experienced the pleasures of the flesh, we know how soon the moment passes and the state of seemingly infinite bliss is over. We were created for permanence but we deceive ourselves and yearn for what is temporary.

Our very reason for existence is to live in eternal communion with God in love, it is why we were made. It is in this, our permanent joy is found and if it isn't, we have not yet understood why we are here. This joy far transcends our wants and our desires. Furthermore, it is in his glorification that we understand the true meaning of satisfaction. Pope John Paul 2 says "What we really seek is

Jesus, the joy for which we yearn is meant to come from him." Oftentimes, though, because we don't quiet our hearts to hear his voice, the voice of the world is magnified. So instead of choosing to 'love' as the word says, we choose to 'use' as the world says. Essentially, it comes down to how attentive we are to the voice of God in our life; if the voice of God is faint then service to him can seem like a restriction to the freedom of satisfying our pleasures. However, if the voice of God resonates loudly in our spirits, we understand that what we consider pleasure is but a mere foretaste of what is to come and true freedom is in Christ. As stated previously, the enemy deceives, so he convinces us all to turn the glory that is due to God to him or inwardly to ourselves. This includes convincing us that God imprisons our desires and that freedom is found in sin, when precisely the opposite is true.

Let's consider the deception from the very start - God gave Adam and Eve everything with one boundary. The devil, cunning as he is, convinced them both that they did not need this boundary and sin entered the world. Fast forward two thousand years, the new Adam; Jesus the one who has come to break the power of sin and death in the world, establishes new boundaries and the devil continues to deceive the world and convince us that those boundaries are a restriction to our freedom yet again. An interesting distortion can be seen with rising acceptance and promotion of abortion. Jesus in the last supper uttered the words "This is my body and my blood" to signify us partaking of his flesh and blood every time we share in Holy Communion. The same words 'This is my body' are now uttered by Pro-choice activists illustrating that they can do what they want with their body. Jesus' message was one of selflessness, the latter, one of selfishness.

It is precisely in these subtle ways that the devil has woven his way into the minds and hearts of the contemporary culture and because the voice and words of God are dormant in many of our lives, arguments which please our every whim progressively sound more plausible.

In addition, what do we draw from the term "my personal life"? Do we own our life? Did we bring ourselves here? Do we know when our last breath will be? Many times we attempt to give ourselves this type of power in an attempt to validate the authority we believe we have over our own lives. The very thought of submission to a being of higher power is a tough pill to swallow especially for men who are innately designed to lead. I would suggest, however, that the more we realize that our life is not our own and that we are part of a divine story which God is ultimately using to fulfill and reward us infinitely out of an unconditional love for us, the easier we can begin to renew our mind towards an eternal perspective.

So be perfect, just as your Father in heaven is perfect. Matthew 5:48

How can God expect us to be perfect? We are not Jesus! To say that Jesus is the model by which we live our lives is a statement very grand in nature indeed. We may be tempted to say that Jesus overcame all that he had to because he was God. However, in reading Paul's letter to the Philippians, we are told that he emptied himself of his divinity while on earth, therefore Jesus did all he had to on earth fully embracing his humanity. So how then did Jesus live a sinless, perfect life if he clung to his human nature? We defined sin in its very essence as simply choosing our own will instead of the Father's. The opposite must then also be true. Overcoming sin, then, is choosing the Father's will over our own consistently whenever the opportunity presents itself. To overcome sin, however, there must be the temptation or opportunity to sin; therefore to remain perfect, Jesus would have had to face temptation of every kind and choose the Father's will every time.

How tremendous is this feat? Let us look at our own life and at how easy the world convinces us to choose our own will. Let us reflect on the last twenty four hours, how many times have we chosen to please ourselves rather than choose to please God? Did you decide to work less hours and receive the same salary? Did you feel that the homeless person didn't need that last five dollars in your wallet? Did you feel that revenge was needed when you were treated unfairly? Did you give in to that temptation of lust? Were you jealous because you were overlooked or slighted for someone else? These few simple examples have one thing in common. They all focus on the 'self' and pleasing or validating 'self'. However, to live as Christ lived is to recognize that the 'self' is created for God. Jesus' actions always pointed to the Father first before himself and thus he was blessed. Similarly, all of our actions must point to Jesus before they point to us. We need God. God doesn't need us as many of us may believe but out of his love, we exist. It is therefore infinitely much less about us than it is about him. We are all pieces in his story, pieces that are infinitely loved by him. Perfection, then is simply recognizing this love that God has for us and out of our love for him, choosing what pleases him consistently, recognizing that that is in fact what is best for us.

I say this knowing fully well how insurmountable it can feel, especially in a world where virtue is shunned and vice is glorified. One recommendation I would give is to shorten our timeframe of reference. For example, it is quite easy to become overwhelmed thinking about the weight of living an entire life pleasing to God. However, our life is not promised; we are not guaranteed seventy or eighty years of life as we may assume. Start with today! Ask yourself what are the decisions that you can make today to allow your relationship with God to grow? What are the toxic habits that you need to cut? Who are the people you need to spend less time with or cut off altogether? What are the situations you need to stop placing yourself in? Apply it to today. If today is still too overwhelming, apply it for the next hour or the next minute? You get the point?

When someone is told they are dying, the plane of focus becomes shortened and magnified because they are now faced with their own mortality. Guess what, you are dying and so am I! Don't wait for a diagnosis to shift your focus into enriching each day of your life. One of the greatest regrets I've heard expressed by persons over the age of sixty five was the length of time they spent pursuing meaningless pleasures in their youth as opposed to doing things that could have added value and meaning to their lives.

Start now, before it's too late. The journey to earthly perfection can only start today. Tomorrow is not promised.

The thief comes only to steal and kill and destroy. I have come so that they may have life and have it to the full. John 10:10

The thief referred to here is the enemy who has one sole purpose: obtaining our souls and preventing us from entering into an eternal relationship with Jesus Christ. The gospel of Matthew highlights that the road to eternal life is narrow and few find it but the road to eternal destruction is wide and many take it. If we do not actively seek out a personal relationship with Jesus through his Holy Spirit, it is very easy and almost guaranteed to find ourselves on the wide road. The devil is cunning. Although he is highlighted in the scripture above as a thief and a killer, he is also vastly deceptive beyond our intellect and makes particularly enticing offers which we may even attribute to God. He has mocked everything God had in store for us from the beginning of time. From the very start, he persuaded Eve to question God and sadly he continues to convince many of us to do the same today. The minute a negative circumstance befalls us, we blame God, but if we obtain a blessing or financial breakthrough, we attribute it to hard work or luck. Quite a convenient belief system. Again if we look at the story of Adam and Eve, God tells them exactly what they need to do to live forever with him. The devil deceives and mankind disobeys.

The scripture highlights particularly that in Christ there is fullness of life, a concept that we ought to grasp in its context. We must first understand that what we consider life and what Christ considers life are on opposing ends of the spectrum. We cling to life, possibly ninety years on earth if we're blessed enough, but a life marred with betrayal, hurt, jealousy, envy, disappointment, frustration, sadness, loneliness, brokenness, depression, hypocrisy, corruption, murder, war, racism, sexual vice, exploitation. Granted there are several glimpses of joy and satisfaction in between, as we examine the list, it is difficult trying to understand to what exactly do we try so hard to cling. Jesus offers us life in a much deeper way, one which transcends all the joys and trials we can imagine. A life without death nor any of the aforementioned. A life where love is manifested through the beatific vision of the triune God on the throne in the presence of his beautiful creation. A life where there is eternal peace and joy and the heavenly choirs fill the air with the praises of God. A life where the church universal is united in the company of the angels and the saints. A life where humanity meets divinity and grace is perfected. This is the LIFE that we must strive for. This is the LIFE that must motivate us. This must be the goal, and if it isn't, sadly we have missed the point of it all.

Many secularists accuse believers of a type of escapism where we cling to a hope of life after death to make the pangs of this life easier to bear but I propose it is much deeper than that. The life of the believer is not merely an escape hatch and it aches me when I hear these unintelligible discussions of matters of faith. If any of us, secular or religious, would take the time to study ourselves, we will discover that we are wired for more than this life. All of the excesses that the world offers still leave us with a longing inside for more. Despite financial status has a man ever expressed that he is completely satisfied with his life? Has one ever expressed that he desires nothing more than his current state? Belief is not merely an escape from the trials of daily life but a blueprint that explains what exactly this daily life means in the context of why we were created. If we were simply animalistic, we would be satisfied with fulfilling our needs and could not care less about words like purpose or meaning. But something within us raises the bar, something tells us that our lives are more than the satisfaction of pleasures, the achievement of goals or the pursuit of relationships. The heart orients itself to God, faith fills the void and Christ provides the fullness of life described above.

As we navigate through the rough seas of this life, let us always bear at the forefront of our mind that there is something infinitely greater which awaits us, which many before us have attained. If we could understand fully the joy and perfection that awaits us, we would echo the words of the beloved St Augustine "Our hearts are restless until they rest in you", and we would understand that everything the world offers is either a distraction or a glimpse of the goal of eternal salvation. We must stay focused on the goal of sainthood; we were bought at too costly a price.

..But you will receive power when the Holy Spirit comes on you then you will be my witnesses not only in Jerusalem but throughout Judea, Samaria and to the ends of the earth. Acts 1:8

Two salient points which are emphasized here are the importance of waiting and the very real transformative power of the Holy Spirit. Something was necessary before the apostles could become witnesses of Jesus to the ends of the earth - the baptism in the Holy Spirit. It highlights the importance of timing and preparation. The responsibility of preaching the message of Jesus and witnessing to his divinity is not an event that should be treated casually. It requires divine assistance because there is divine opposition. It also points to the danger of entering specific avenues in life without being adequately prepared. At the end of the gospels, the apostles were broken and afraid, still trying to come to terms with the death of their leader and close friend, completely unprepared and ill-equipped to proclaim a message of salvation to hearts in need. Many times we choose to enter specific paths for which we are not ready. I have observed many individuals who adopt a super Christian approach and try to force Jesus upon others from a place of superiority. While God has given all believers a firm instruction to spread the good news to all, it has to be under the anointing of the Holy Spirit otherwise the goal will always be to win an argument. The goal should ultimately be to win souls but only God can do that through us. Therefore we need to be astute at recognizing the voice of the spirit moving within us before we make any moves towards evangelization, counsel or any life decision. I have seen the most articulate arguments rendered useless in bringing someone to Christ; ironically, I have also seen the simplest statements resonate profoundly and bring about conviction and conversion. The difference? The Holy Spirit. One points to God's glory, the other points to our own. We must always be careful in our walk that we are not doing things to glorify our own ego as it is easy to get caught up in one's own gifts and abilities, forgetting the source of them.

Jesus in his wisdom knew the transformative and life giving power of the Holy Spirit which is why he encouraged the apostles to wait in Acts 1:8. The effects were witnessed days later at Pentecost in the upper room. The Holy Spirit came with power and it is almost as if the apostles shed their cocoons of fear and iniquity and were filled with joy and boldness. Immediately following, Peter preached to a crowd convicting and baptizing three thousand, days later, five thousand. The Holy Spirit magnifies what we think we can do and achieve. We often have our own plans and intentions but with a little patience, the spirit of God transforms our situation to an entirely different playing field. Once we submit, we move from the realm of human strengths and weaknesses which are finite and enter the realm of an omnipotent God whose power and reach are infinite.

When we operate under the anointing of God's Holy Spirit it also shifts the way we view others. We no longer see people by their actions or words but by their hearts, which is essentially how God views us. We naturally focus on the external: words, deeds, features, race and class. God, however, simplifies the equation quite plainly. Let us strive to operate in his realm.

The Spirit gives life; the flesh counts for nothing. The words I have spoken to you— they are full of the Spirit and life. John 6:63

It is easy to become consumed by what the flesh has to offer. We are exposed after all to everything that appeals to our senses on a daily basis. This word highlights to us that reading scripture is not simply an exercise like studying a particular subject. The words written are transformative and life giving because they are the words of Christ. What do we mean though when we say the phrase 'The words of Christ? Let us pause here for a second so we can appreciate the magnitude of this statement. Let us try to conceive that before this universe began, in a realm which we do not fully understand, God existed: Father, Son and Spirit. We know this from Genesis 1. God made a world for us to exist in love with him. Along the way through our free decisions, we chose to act in our best interest instead of doing that which pleased God. Through this self-serving decision making, quite a mess was made and sin entered the world. With sin came the consequence of sin which is death. God, existing outside of time, knew the world needed redemption and that we needed saving from our consequences so he chose to send his son, Jesus, out of love for us. Science has progressed enough to illustrate to us how vast the universe is, and that the planet earth is a speck of dust in the grand design of everything that we have come to know. Consider that within the grandeur and splendor of all that God created, he chose to send his son who lived outside of creation so that we too may be able to one day share in the existence which they do outside of time, space and creation.

This is the perspective we must have when reading the words of Jesus. We must try to read as best as possible with his eyes, his mind, his love, though we cannot fully relate. There is a reason why faith is ignited within us when the words of Jesus penetrate our heart and soul. There is a reason why those who believe completely in his words are deeply committed to spreading these words to the ends of the earth. It is because they have become fully aware that this life is but a shadow, an iota, a miniscule dot in all that is to come for those who believe. This is why the words of Jesus are not merely words of encouragement. They are much more because they open the door to a world that is far grander, far beyond anything that our senses can conceptualize. They are spirit and they are life. They have the capacity to transform us into who we really should be. It is why the saints lived with such a burning passion for eternity - a desire to put the love of Christ above the love of everything else understanding that it is out of his love for us and our love for him that every source of joy and perfect peace emanates. St Thérèse of Lisieux strived to make herself 'small' and be carried by God through this life. She did this because she came to the realization and understanding of the tremendous love and grace which is the driving force to take us to the end. It is as if his grace provides the elevator to the top but our human will is the staircase. Both may take us to the same place but we are incredibly more likely to get weary using the staircase especially when the journey takes us to great heights.

Let us strive then to see beyond. Take his words for what they are. His words are not meant to simply be read as a novel or a motivational tool, it greatly transcends this. They are in fact words which penetrate flesh, soul and spirit and transform us into who we are called to be. The truth is we have but a few decades here on this earth to figure this out. Yet it is the single most important fact that we can come to appreciate in this life. It is so important that the creator himself felt it necessary to become as we are, pay a price for all of our shortcomings and illuminate our eyes to the fact that there is more to what we experience here. Let us then be ignited to live within this perspective and understanding.

Reflections on Perspective

- Do I have an eternal perspective on my life?

- Can I look beyond my current situation?

- Do I recognize that God is bigger than my problems and trials?

- Do I find myself looking for satisfaction is everything/everybody else but God?

Affirmations

- The longing I have inside can only be satisfied by God.

- I am made for eternity.

- I will evaluate the decisions in my life with eternity in mind.

VICTORY

"...For your sake we face death all day long; we are considered as sheep to be slaughtered." No, in all these things we are more than conquerors through him who loved us. Romans 8:36-37

Daily life can be seen as a battle by many and indeed it is. The Christian life for what it's worth is nothing short of a daily battle until the very moment we take our last breath. Let us pause here briefly.

The US Navy Sea, Air and Land Teams (SEALs) are a special branch of armed defense trained in tactical weaponry to eliminate specific deadly targets. They are considered by many to be the most elite tactical unit on the planet. To put this into perspective, it was the US Navy SEALs who were responsible for the intricate reconnaissance mission which led to the assassination of Osama Bin Laden in 2011. To create these mental machines, Navy SEALs endure some of the most inhumane training, pushing the body to absolute mental and physical limits in a variety of horrific environments. The training is designed to teach the recruits that there is an enemy on the other side who is relentless in the pursuit of their lives. SEALs train understanding that they are pushed beyond these limits because on the battlefield, there are no breaks or let downs. The enemy doesn't stop when there is fatigue or weakness. The enemy only stops when they are defeated.

There is a lot to be learned from the mental conditioning that the SEALs endure within the context of Romans 8:36-37 above. SEALs are trained to fight from advantageous, strategic positions, often defeating their enemies with surprise espionage attacks from within, such as with the case of Osama Bin Laden. SEALs were dropped off at Bin Laden's residence in Pakistan close to midnight on May 2nd, 2011. However this was as a result of the CIA closely monitoring and evaluating the most strategic time for the drop off months prior. Mock designs of the compound were made so that SEALs trained and knew the exact structure of the building, entrances and exits and also exactly where Osama would be, the third floor of his compound in Pakistan.

On May 1st, 2011 the small group of three SEALs were dropped off at Osama's base, confident but understanding the gravity of the situation and the likelihood of being shot and killed upon sight. Unfazed, the men entered stealthily making their way up to the third floor of the house blowing their way through the doors, eliminating any enemies in the process. By the time they got to the third floor, Osama was so surprised of the attack that the only line of defense for him was to grab his youngest wife and hide behind her. It was then that Robert O'Neil shot him twice in the forehead and killed him. This was the moment, the purpose of the rigorous training, the months of preparation and reconnaissance, the nerves and anxiety, but also the do or die mentality that they were going to enter that compound, conquer and leave. What is the significance of the death of one of the world's former leading terrorists?

There were many things that could have gone wrong in the mission. If the men's cover had been blown before time, they would all have been dead. Had they not prepared, they may have never found him. Most importantly, if they did not believe that they were fighting a battle they could win, they would never have even picked up a weapon.

The sad reality is many of us don't prepare for the spiritual battles we face daily, even though Jesus tells us that the journey is long and we will suffer just as he did. Many of us don't train and evaluate how well equipped we are to defeat the enemy. Just as the SEALs could not enter the physical battle unprepared, so too, we cannot enter our daily spiritual battles unprepared. We need to be filled with the words of Christ as our foundation and live in communion with him through his Holy Spirit, recognizing his authority and reign. Finally, and most importantly, we must fight *knowing* we have an advantage. We have already won the victory through Jesus' death and resurrection. Let us not reduce what Jesus did by fooling ourselves into thinking that it is an even fight. We do not trade blows with the enemy as if this is a closely contested bout. It is much different. The battle is already WON. We have our feet on his neck, but we let up, because he convinces us that we are not strong enough. Make no mistake saints, Satan has been defeated eternally, but he needs to be continue to be defeated daily by your cooperation with faith and your trust in God's grace. Press into his word and prayer daily and keep him down and if you're Catholic, lean into the intercession of the saints and the Blessed Virgin Mary!

Sometimes however, we give the enemy too much credit. We must be strategic, identify our areas of weakness and play to our strengths. I understand that at times many of us may have sinful habits that are difficult to break and may require help and advice from a third party but I also believe that there are many practical steps we know we can take to start intelligently earning our victory in Christ.

The following is a basic example: if you know every time you spend time alone with your significant other, the result is fornication, don't blame the devil; rather, blame your naivety. You are not fighting from a strategic point, but a defeated point, carrying a knife to a gun battle. We must actively spend time understanding ourselves, our triggers and moments of weakness and turn them into strengths.

Only when we submit to his spirit of wisdom to guide our decisions then we will fight with a serious advantage. We are not simply meant to casually survive our daily battles. Just as the SEALs were strategic and conquered, we are called to be MORE than conquerors so let us spiritually train, plan, strategize and conquer as such!

I do not understand what I do. For what I want to do I do not do, but what I hate I do. And if I do what I do not want to do, I agree that the law is good. As it is, it is no longer I myself who do it, but it is sin living in me. For I know that good itself does not dwell in me, that is, in my sinful nature. **Romans 7:15-18**

The first time I ever read this scripture I was about twenty one years old and it struck me like a bolt of lightning with its accuracy. One could only imagine the initial response of the Romans when first reading this letter from Paul. Some probably considered him to be a man so carnal and unrestricted in his desires that he seemed no different from an animal. Others may have related quite seamlessly. I believe, if we are honest with ourselves, the latter would be the majority and we, through a little introspection, would easily find ourselves there. We all undergo the same battle that Paul articulates so clearly to the Romans. We all battle against the sin that lives within us and sometimes that battle can seem hopeless when we become enveloped in the weight of our sin.

It is important to remember that all of the saints who have walked before us all struggled intensely with internal sin. In fact, that is precisely what made them saints. There can be no virtue if there is no circumstance where sin is an option. Virtue lies in being faced with sin and righteousness, and choosing righteousness consistently. This, essentially is the call of the Christian: to choose righteousness consistently until death when we are perfected in grace in eternal life.

However, this is easier said than done and I am far from purporting to be an expert in this field. I find myself as many of us should, in the words of Paul in this chapter, where we do the wrong thing which we hate and do not do the right thing which we know to be right. It is important, however, to focus on Paul's response. Although it seems as a desperate cry of being a sinful man unworthy of God's mercy, he ends the discourse by saying, "who will rescue me from this wretched body? Thanks be to God through Christ Jesus" Romans 7:25.

In this short monologue, Paul highlights our template for our battle against sin. We will feel overwhelmed, overburdened and unworthy. Thankfully God's mercy is not characterized by how we feel about ourselves and that is a point we need to keep at the forefront of our minds. The blueprint for victory is in recognizing that within ourselves, we are ill-equipped to overcome our fleshly desires, but we have access to the one whose strength and grace is infinite, and who is willing and able to dispense grace as needed to overcome all of the challenges we will ever face. He wants us all to recognize that we are not defined by our weaknesses, shortcomings, failures and consistent disappointments but rather by the many outlets of grace that Jesus offers once we turn to him with contrite hearts.

I do not find anything to boast of within myself, but I acknowledge fully that my ability to journey towards salvation and encourage others to do the same stems solely from a daily outpouring of Jesus' grace upon my life.

One of the deadliest lies Satan has convinced us to believe is that we are self-sufficient and have no need for any supernatural "help" from God and many have drunk this deadly poison. If we can learn anything from the saints whose lives we are called to emulate, we notice one consistent theme - they all understood clearly the importance of prayer.

St Dominic spent all night in prayer to preach all day with very little rest. St Angela of Foligno would spend hours of contemplative prayer in front of her crucifix. St. Catherine of Siena, at the beginning of her conversion, spent three years in her own room praying intensely in silence and solitude. The church has declared these men and women exemplary in their victory over personal sin by the way they lived their lives because they understood the effort it took to live victoriously.

Our lives may not afford all of us the luxury of spending entire days in prayer but we must recognize the need for it and allocate sufficient time. The bigger the trial, the greater the prayer and grace needed. Prayer invites God into the situation, it welcomes grace which the church teaches is our supernatural aid. We were not meant to overcome our burdens alone. Peter says in 1 Peter 5:7 "Cast all your burdens upon him, for he cares about you." We were designed to be reliant on grace to be sustained. The frustration arises when we try to do it without grace. Think of a scuba diver going into the Atlantic Ocean without an oxygen tank. Most trained Navy SEALs can hold their breath for approximately two to three minutes, if one's life depended on it, maybe a little longer. Soon enough, however, no matter how hard the diver tries his lungs will collapse and require oxygen. Think of God's grace as our oxygen tank: no matter how hard we try, there will be failure, disappointment and frustration at some point. However, just as an oxygen tank gives us the tools needed to dive into the deepest seas, so too does God's grace equip us to face the most challenging temptations and trials. God has given us the tools needed. Let us equip ourselves!

The following question should now be at the forefront of your mind: "How do I receive God's grace?"

Luckily it's not too hard. We can start right now.

Step 1

Take a moment to reflect. Try to think of every morally wrong thing you *know* you have done. Then seek further help by downloading an 'Examination of Conscience' online.

Step 2

After thoroughly examining the wrongs in your life, if you are Catholic you should visit the nearest priest and obtain the sacrament of Reconciliation. Grace is provided through this sacrament instituted by Jesus for the forgiveness of sin. If not, you can try to make a sincere act of contrition and ask God for his mercy and grace to overcome whatever struggle you may have.

Step 3

Develop a solid prayer life. Spend quality time in prayer. Talk to God but also listen! Build an intimate relationship with him. Grace is poured out as we pray in humility. In our prayer we must avidly recognize that we are fragile, at best, without God and that we are infinitely dependent on him for our very existence. Prayer in humility welcomes God's grace and that grace leads to victory.

Step 4

Charity. Jesus left us two commandments in Matthew 22: "You shall love the Lord your God with all your heart, and with all your soul, and with all your mind. This is the first and greatest commandment. And the second is like unto it, you shall love your neighbour as yourself."

The second commandment flows out of the first. We show our love for God by the way we treat his creation. *All* of his creation, including the ones that are the most difficult to love. Dorothy Day gives us a beautiful reminder of this when she says "I only love God as much as the person I love the least." It is always a clear wake up call for me that we do not have the option of choosing who we love. Intimacy, yes, but not love, we are required to love all, meaning we are required to will the good of all.

It is a reminder that the Christian life is not insular, it is by its very nature selfless because the founder himself committed the most selfless act by giving his very life for all. How much more then must we give of ourselves to those in need! Great grace is given to those who do good with a pure heart. Peter tells us in fact that "Above all, love each other deeply because love covers over a multitude of sins." 1 Peter 4:8

Step 5
Attend Mass as often as you can!
There is no greater intimacy with Jesus than receiving him, Body, Blood, Soul and Divinity. He said so himself in the gospel of John ""In all truth I tell you, if you do not eat the flesh of the Son of man and drink his blood, you have no life in you."

These aren't my words. They are his. If we want life, we must want him on his terms not ours.

"..But since you are neither hot nor cold, but only lukewarm, I will spit you out of my mouth." Revelation 3:16

It is quite common for many to be incredibly selective of particular verses in the Bible to suit our lifestyle. The fact is that God's mercy will always be more popular than his justice because it is easier for us to accept. The thought of a God who loves us and will forgive our wrong doings is far more palatable than a God who will eternally punish us for our wrong doing. In order for us to understand and achieve victory, however, we must understand both mercy and justice and how it relates to our salvation.

We must understand that Jesus' act of dying on the cross was the perfect act of agape love. His decision to will the good of humanity by dying in the most inhumane manner, taking the weight of the sin of the world upon himself then conquering death through resurrection is the blueprint for our victory today. To sin is not merely to do what we want, but on a larger scale, it is to deny this perfect act of love, to reject his selfless act and the immeasurable gift of salvation. He tells us in John 14 that he must go to prepare a place for us so that where he goes, we may also be. To sin is not just to turn our backs on him but also on every one of his promises. This is where the scope of his justice is introduced. Jesus will not force eternal life upon us. If we lived a life for ourselves which denied everything which Jesus offered then it would certainly be unjust at the end for God to force his will upon us and force us to be with him. It would contradict the very nature of his creating us to freely choose him, if at the end he eliminates this choice and forces a decision upon us. In a sense, then, if we do not inherit eternal life, it is not because God did not love us enough to save us, but because we did not love him enough to accept the free gift which he offered.

Now where does being lukewarm fit into this equation? When one is lukewarm he is neither for God nor for himself; there is no allegiance, only a perpetual vacillation. This is dangerous because it not only shows God that we understand his standard and choose to reject it at our convenience but it also gives a false representation of the faith to others who may see indecisiveness as the example which we are called to emulate. This falsely represents the faith which Jesus expects of us. We either serve God with everything we have or we do not. Nothing less than his standard is acceptable simply because he did not give us a half-hearted effort in opening the gate to salvation; he gave all he could possibly give. Only by understanding and choosing to give this effort towards his standard will victory be achieved. The devil is fully committed to robbing us of the gift of salvation because he has limited time left. We cannot then inherit eternal life with a half-hearted effort, it simply won't work. We need to recognize the battle that exists and fight fully for our salvation which has been purchased for us. Warriors who fight half-heartedly never attain victory.

Blessed be the God and Father of our Lord Jesus Christ, who has blessed us in Christ with every spiritual blessing in the heavenly places, even as he chose us in him before the foundation of the world, that we should be holy and blameless before him. In love he predestined us for adoption to himself as sons through Jesus Christ, according to the purpose of his will, to the praise of his glorious grace, with which he has blessed us in the Beloved. Ephesians 1: 3-6

The above scripture is excellent at reminding us that through Jesus we have received every spiritual blessing required to have victory. Let us reflect on these words. Every. Spiritual. Blessing. Could it be that every single element of heaven, every bit of power, grace, mercy, strength, talent, gift that can possibly be given to us, has been given to us? Very simply put, yes. God has given everything he can give to us. The creator of everything has given us everything we need so that we may return to him to be eternally joyful and at peace. Jesus has not held back anything from us for our salvation to be made possible. This and only this is salvation and God's divine plan for us. This is why he echoes these words to us in John 14:6 after Thomas asks "Lord, we do not know where you are going, how can we know the way?" and Jesus responds "I am the way, the truth and the life." Jesus was essentially highlighting that though there may be many paths that seemingly lead to many different destinations, he is the only way which can lead to the destination that he has prepared for us.

Victory and salvation do not simply exist in a distant place that we go to when we die and are judged; it starts right here the moment we repent and accept Jesus Christ as the Lord of our lives. This is where eternal life begins (John 17:3). Recognizing this plays a major role in establishing victory because we recognize the devil's traps and temptations for what they are and we understand the beauty of the life that we are forsaking when we chose to give into his temptations rather than live in the purity and peace of God's grace. It is important to recognize that God has sent from heaven every spiritual blessing for us because he knows how excruciatingly difficult achieving eternal life can sometimes feel with all of the challenges that this life has to offer, but focusing on the difficulty of the task at hand does not make it any easier to bear.

The Harvard University Department of Mathematics describes Math 55 as "probably the most difficult undergraduate math class in the country". Students cover four semesters of work in a year which is certainly an insurmountable task for many. It is even widely regarded as the most difficult undergraduate math course in the world. Consider the following facts about the course before we continue:

1. The size of the class drops by 50% by the end
2. Problem sets take 24-60 hours per week to complete
3. Students present 15-20 pages of work per problem set
4. Most students develop insomnia due to the incredible work load
5. Easy problems generally take approximately an hour and a half to answer
6. Due to the intense structure you cannot double major if you're enrolled in the course
7. Approximately 50% of Math 55 students go on to become professors

'Ameya A. Velingker took Advanced Placement calculus his freshman year and ranked in the top 12 for the USA Math Olympiad the year after that. "It was a tough decision to drop," Velingker says. "You're around all these people who are beasts at math. But I realized it was not going to work out."'

Now what is the relationship between Math 55 and our daily Christian journey? Well on the surface it may not seem like much and you may be wondering why I decided to insert this seemingly obscure example but upon closer examination, the similarities are glaring.

Let us examine the points above again a little deeper:

1. **The size of the class drops by 50% by the end-** There are many who will start the Christian journey but will not remain for many reasons. As highlighted by Jesus in the parable of the sower and the seed, some may hear the word and not understand it, others will hear the word but the trials of life will be too much to bear and others will hear the word but the enticements of this world will be too attractive for them to refuse.

   Interestingly enough, just as the professors know that 50% of the class will not complete the course, Jesus also knows sadly, that many will fail their final examination upon judgement. He expresses this in Matt 7:14 *"But small is the gate and narrow the road that leads to life, and only a few find it."* He is aware that many will refuse to accept all of the gifts he has bestowed upon us to embrace our call to eternal life. But just as professors will not force students to stay and receive the tools required to succeed, similarly Jesus will not impose his will upon us either. He will simply present us with the option of eternal life, the grace needed to achieve it and his Spirit to guide us along the way. He will also reveal to us at different points in our journey glimpses of the beauty of communion in him. He never leaves us or abandons but one thing is certain, he will not make your choices for you. If after all of his efforts to empower, comfort, redeem and sanctify you, you still decide he is not worth it, then you have chosen to live outside of communion with him and that is irreversible after you have received the failing grade on your exam.

2. **Problem sets take 24-60 hours per week to complete-** Many of the trials that we will undergo will require

patience and some sort of sacrifice. We may be able to overcome some quickly through prayer and faith but others we will need to endure like Job. I will use the writing of this book as an example. This project has taken over three years to complete. There were times I stopped writing for months due to discouragement or when I simply did not feel very inspired to do so. However I could not ignore the call that was placed on my heart to complete it. So as many late nights and early mornings that were required, the sacrifice was made because I know the good that God intended to come out of it.

Many of the blessings that you have for the world will require great effort and sacrifice before they come to fruition. Remember part of our imitation of Christ's life is the way in which we emulate his sacrifice and suffering therefore, at some point you must ask yourself if you will be part of the many who will give up and refuse to sacrifice for something greater or be a part of the few who will endure and be victorious and achieve the fruit that God has intended for yourself and the world.

3. **Students present 15-20 pages of work per problem set-**Fall in love with the process. The trials that we undergo are excellent at developing temerity and an abundance of other gifts that bring about spiritual, emotional, mental and physical growth. Essentially, nothing simply happens to us. We are the sum total of the decisions we may make and choosing to live the life that Christ calls us to is the only way we will ever fully become the person we are ultimately called to be. He

knows us better than we know ourselves and he is fully aware of the fruit that we have to offer to the world. Our 'yes' to him opens doors and opportunities that we hardly could have ever achieved on our own.

4. **Most students develop insomnia due to the incredible work load-** An entire section of this book is devoted to suffering. We will suffer, in some way. We will all have different experiences in our journey but rest assured that victory will come. We must remind ourselves though that they are not an end in themselves but a valiant tool of growth and development in every chapter of the journey if we choose to embrace it.

5. **Due to the intense structure you cannot double major if you're enrolled in the course-** One of the biggest stumbling blocks we have in our Christian journey is the fact that we often live dual lives. There's an intelligent reason why Harvard doesn't allow double majors once enrolled in Math 55. They understand the rigor of work required, the sacrifice, the long hours, the commitment. They understand that the course must be their priority while enrolled for them to be even remotely successful. There is little that could be more profoundly accurate about Christianity than this!

Similar to our Christian journey, there's a clear reason why Jesus says if we are neither hot nor cold, he will spit us out. We cannot double major our Christian life with the life we want unless the two are in alignment. Sadly, most of us try to live this contradiction daily from time to time, myself included. It takes a perpetual dying to self, daily, to be completely open to the voice of God, and being attentive to his will upon your life. Interestingly enough, once we realize what that will is, we realize why we cannot balance it with anything else because it demands our entire selves. Serving God requires our lives, our time, our *full* effort. It is not an extra-curricular activity that we engage in on Sunday morning, neither is it meeting a particular requirement of obedience one day a week. It is a decision that if taken seriously permeates all facets of our lives.

As mentioned previously, when we consider what we're up against, we understand why we must be relentless and focused in our approach towards salvation. The church teaches us that we fight against three enemies that do not leave us until the moment of death. These are: the flesh, the world, the devil.

The flesh describes the battle within. This was discussed this previously in Romans 7. Paul explains how he fights arduously against his own sinful nature which pulls him towards sin. We inherited this original sin from our first parents Adam and Eve.

This internal battle is clearly different from the external temptations that we face from the other two enemies we will discuss subsequently. We can all relate to Paul in this particular scripture as we all battle with being torn with the urges and temptations of the flesh within and trying to do what we know to be right. Oftentimes though, there is the tendency to associate sins of the flesh only with sexual sin, but our mortal urges are many: greed, the urge to seek revenge, withhold forgiveness, selfishly withhold information. The mind acting upon impulse will invariably prompt the body to act in a manner that causes the greatest immediate pleasure to the self. Without self-control, however, this can be abused and the abuses of this often bring with it dire consequences. Think of satisfying our need for hunger: when we are hungry, chemical reactions in the body prompt us to satisfy that urge by eating. Without self-control, however, we can easily abuse this and eat considerably more than we need to, causing harm to our bodies resulting in symptoms such as diarrhoea or vomiting. The effect becomes even more extreme when we consider abuses like the quest for power. Most of us are required to work to earn a living, the abuses of that can lead to greed and corruption, causing income inequality and relative poverty. The abuse of our sexual desires can lead to promiscuity, resulting in deadly consequences such as sexually transmitted diseases, abortions and subsequent death.

From the examples, we understand that all our desires were made to be fulfilled within particular boundaries, however, once these boundaries are violated, we begin to understand the physical, emotional and spiritual consequences of our actions.

The world refers to the many temptations all around that may prompt us to act in a sinful manner. It is opposite to the flesh in that the immediate battle is not within, the temptations are external to us. One may interject here that temptation is all around, so what must the Christian do but live in a bubble? Unfortunately this is preached from some pulpits but it is not the message preached by Jesus. We must understand the dichotomy which exists here. We are called to be in the world but not of the world. The world is where we live, we cannot escape it; however, we must recognize that our presence must impact the world around us and not the other way around. We are called to be a light in the darkness. This is where our victory lies, we must recognize that within us lies the same power that dwelled within Christ - the power to convict and transform hearts - and this is our mission. Understand, however, that this does not mean we will blindly go to all places under the guise of evangelism. We must be guided by the Spirit since it is the Spirit who convicts. Many end up lost by trying to be a part of everything with the good intention of setting an example, only to end up falling prey to the world's enticements. Good intentions are naive at best if not guided by the Spirit of God.

Additionally, we must recognize the power of our senses. There is a reason why at Christmas time at the malls, there is music, elegant decorations and even particular smells of Christmas food. Our senses guide our behavior. A study done by Donovan and Rossiter, 1982 highlight that a store's atmosphere actually affects the emotional state of its consumers. By controlling the tempo, pitch and volume of songs in various stores, store owners actually control the pleasure centers of the brain responsible for releasing dopamine, oxytocin and serotonin and cause shoppers to behave in different ways. Brainwashing at its finest. Consider this the next time you go Christmas shopping. The example in this instance may seem unrelated but the fact is that there are many factors in our world that trigger us to act in a manner unbecoming of ourselves and in fact leave us brainwashed. I'm certain we can recall various instances where we have found ourselves in various situations doing things that we hardly ever expected simply because of the outward pressures and influences that were in our space at the time. Unfortunately, many are swept with the tide because they overlook how serious the pull of the world can be. Recognizing the external battle is critical to winning it.

The devil, the third enemy, is probably the most popular and definitely the most blamed! He is also the most powerful. He is not simply some imaginary red being with a pitchfork, horns and a tail waiting for us in the pits of hell. We must develop a much more mature understanding than that. Scripture tells us in Rev 12:9 that when Lucifer betrayed Jesus in the heavens, he and all of his angels were hurled down to earth. Not hell as popularly conceived, but **earth**. In addition, scripture is also quite clear on his purpose while on earth in 1 Peter 5:8. It says the enemy, the devil is prowling around like a roaring lion, looking for someone to devour. I believe words like lion and devour are intentionally used as his desire for our souls is not to be taken lightly, it should emphasize the pernicious nature with which he wants to seize ownership of us. He understands that we have an opportunity to have what he can no longer, communion with God.

The enemy's purpose is emphasized so we can completely understand the focus and perspective we ought to have in order to live victoriously. The devil ensures that we will not easily earn our salvation. He is a supernatural being who is incredibly wiser than us who also knows us better than we know ourselves. This means he cleverly knows our strengths and weaknesses and how to manipulate the world and provide temptations to magnify the sinful desires already dwelling within to lead us to the eventual destruction that he will also experience.

St Basil the Great famously says "Hell cannot be made attractive, so the devil makes attractive the road that leads there." The devil will never make the wrong decision seem wrong, he will always manipulate us into thinking that it is the best decision and that there is no consequence for our actions. This is why the words of Christ and the saints are so important. We must continuously remind ourselves of the devil's identity and also condemn him with authority on a daily basis just as Jesus did in the desert.

The father of all lies will never have our best interest at heart regardless of how well packaged the destructive road may seem. Resisting him then must be a consistent action since his schemes are relentless. We must ardently engross ourselves in the word of God which we know to be true and actively live righteous lives through the power of the Holy Spirit.

I have witnessed firsthand the power that the devil has over those who may be possessed or afflicted by evil spirits and it is truly nothing that should be made light of. What is striking is that regardless of the geographical location, the pattern is the same. Over the years I have visited Aruba, Guyana, the US Virgin Islands and as far as Slovenia to do ministry and have seen the same result. The devil enters us through a door that we open, usually through sin or some vice then convinces us that he has to stay. It is sometimes a very difficult task to deliver someone who is spiritually afflicted because their mind has to first be released from the devil's lies. The devil may convince someone that their life is worthless, that no one loves them, that they have no purpose, that they are meant to be stricken by some disease or physical sickness all the days of our life but if we understand the words of Jesus, we know that all of these things are the exact opposite of what Jesus promises us. It is important to note though that it should not be assumed that anyone who experiences some sort of lengthy physical or emotional affliction is under the grip of Satan. Though he is very real, it is always recommended that persons obtain medical and psychiatric checks first to ensure the problems cannot be solved naturally before delving into supernatural help. For further reading on this topic I highly recommend "An Exorcist explains the Demonic: *The Antics of Satan and His fallen angels*" by the renowned Vatican exorcist Fr. Gabriele Amorth.

We know our lives are of value because Jesus died for us while we were still sinners **(*Romans 5:8*)** he didn't wait until we sorted out our lives, but performed the perfect act of agape love by dying for us while we didn't deserve it. This should indicate to us how much our lives are worth to him. He knows the incredible freedom that awaits us should we believe in him and he was willing to sacrifice everything for it, including his own life. This alone points to our worth in his eyes.

We know we are loved based on John 3:16. It tells us "For God so *loved* the world that he gave his only son, that whoever believes in him shall not perish but have everlasting life." Love is the only reason why Jesus did what He did. He didn't do it because it felt like the right thing to do because quite frankly if it was based on a feeling, He would have probably given up in the Garden of Gethsemane. He persevered out of the love and the decision he made to love us even before we were created. What a pity it would be to have the devil feed us a few lies to strip us of the beauty of salvation that awaits us through belief in Jesus.

We all have a purpose. Matthew 5:14 tells us we are called to be the light of the world. Light dispels darkness and we are called to let our light shine regardless of how dark the world may be. There are some people who will only come to freedom and victory through our witness to them, through our light. It is critical that we do not let the darkness of the world and the enemy derail that purpose. It is incredibly easy to feel purposeless in this life, even without the devil's assistance. Life can become quite mundane and routine in nature especially if we do not consistently remind ourselves that our ultimate purpose transcends our daily routine. When we combine this fact with an enemy who knows how to use our daily routine to strip our purpose, we are in for quite a battle. Throughout the routine though, God always provides opportunities for our lights to shine. It may be in the simplest of acts, such as lending an ear to someone who may be going through some dire circumstance or providing a word of encouragement to another. Sometimes all it takes is a word to bring about transformation and conviction within someone's heart. The primary attack of the enemy is in convincing us of his lies over God's promises. Once we equip ourselves with the truth of God's word, we can fully embrace our purpose and we become capable of destroying the enemy and his lies.

One of the main elements of Jesus' ministry was healing. There are countless examples of this taking place in the gospels. One of the main scriptures depicting his healing is in Matthew 15:30 "And large crowds came to him, bringing with them those who were lame, crippled, blind, mute, and many others, and they laid them down at his feet; and he *healed* them." It is clear that Jesus never intends for us to stay in a state of sickness or disease since this is not of him. He desires that we may all be healed and takes joy in our healing. In fact, healing is a true representation of his power. Therefore, we must never believe the lie that we are meant to be sick or stricken by some illness; this again is a lie from the enemy to keep us in bondage and shift our focus from the healing and freedom that Christ has promised. As the tone of this chapter suggests, we must live victoriously and freely in Christ.

Rest assured, we have all we need to achieve the fullness of peace and joy in Christ which we deserve. He has rained down every blessing and gift from the heavens upon us so that we are fully equipped to overcome the difficulties of this life. The question we must ask ourselves is if we are ready to receive it? I know many who are not as fortunate to know the saving power of Jesus. Woe unto those who know the life and promises that he has given us and choose otherwise. Eternity is quite a long time to spend in regret. Let us never forget, the devil may have power, but Jesus has authority! Remind yourselves! Now is the time, choose well saints.

The following is an account of the sin of David. I encourage you to take two to three minutes to read the following before we analyze the many factors that were wrong in this situation besides the apparent 'sin of adultery' which is usually spoken of.

2 Samuel 11

<u>*David and Bathsheba*</u>

1 In the spring, at the time when kings go off to war, David sent Joab out with the king's men and the whole Israelite army. They destroyed the Ammonites and besieged Rabbah. But David remained in Jerusalem.

2 One evening David got up from his bed and walked around on the roof of the palace. From the roof he saw a woman bathing. The woman was very beautiful, 3 and David sent someone to find out about her. The man said, "She is Bathsheba, the daughter of Eliam and the wife of Uriah the Hittite." 4 Then David sent messengers to get her. She came to him, and he slept with her. (Now she was purifying herself from her monthly uncleanness.) Then she went back home. 5 The woman conceived and sent word to David, saying, "I am pregnant."

6 So David sent this word to Joab: "Send me Uriah the Hittite." And Joab sent him to David. 7 When Uriah came to him, David asked him how Joab was, how the soldiers were and how the war was going. 8 Then David said to Uriah, "Go down to your house and wash your feet." So Uriah left the palace, and a gift from the king was sent after him. 9 But Uriah slept at the entrance to the palace with all his master's servants and did not go down to his house.

10 David was told, "Uriah did not go home." So he asked Uriah, "Haven't you just come from a military campaign? Why didn't you go home?"

11 Uriah said to David, "The ark and Israel and Judah are staying in tents, and my commander Joab and my lord's men are camped in the open country. How could I go to my house to eat and drink and make love to my wife? As surely as you live, I will not do such a thing!"

12 Then David said to him, "Stay here one more day, and tomorrow I will send you back." So Uriah remained in Jerusalem that day and the next. 13 At David's invitation, he ate and drank with him, and David made him drunk. But in the evening Uriah went out to sleep on his mat among his master's servants; he did not go home.

14 In the morning David wrote a letter to Joab and sent it with Uriah. 15 In it he wrote, "Put Uriah out in front where the fighting is fiercest. Then withdraw from him so he will be struck down and die."

16 So while Joab had the city under siege, he put Uriah at a place where he knew the strongest defenders were. 17 When the men of the city came out and fought against Joab, some of the men in David's army fell; moreover, Uriah the Hittite died.

18 Joab sent David a full account of the battle. 19 He instructed the messenger: "When you have finished giving the king this account of the battle, 20 the king's anger may flare up, and he may ask you, 'Why did you get so close to the city to fight? Didn't you know they would shoot arrows from the wall? 21 Who killed Abimelek son of Jerub-

Besheth? Didn't a woman drop an upper millstone on him from the wall, so that he died in Thebez? Why did you get so close to the wall?' If he asks you this, then say to him, 'Moreover, your servant Uriah the Hittite is dead.'

²² The messenger set out, and when he arrived he told David everything Joab had sent him to say. ²³ The messenger said to David, "The men overpowered us and came out against us in the open, but we drove them back to the entrance of the city gate. ²⁴ Then the archers shot arrows at your servants from the wall, and some of the king's men died. Moreover, your servant Uriah the Hittite is dead."

²⁵ David told the messenger, "Say this to Joab: 'Don't let this upset you; the sword devours one as well as another. Press the attack against the city and destroy it.' Say this to encourage Joab."

²⁶ When Uriah's wife heard that her husband was dead, she mourned for him. ²⁷ After the time of mourning was over, David had her brought to his house, and she became his wife and bore him a son. But the thing David had done displeased the LORD.

Verse 1 opens with the line "When kings go off to war…", however, we soon realize that *King* David was not present during the current war against the Ammonites. The following verses tell us that he sent his commander Joab off to fight with the Israelite Army. This opening line tells us something about the character of David. Why wasn't David more closely involved in the battle of the men who fought for him? David seems to abdicate his responsibility with no apparent excuse or valid reason and this is understood clearly in verse 2 which says that David got up in the evening and walked around his roof! He did so while the men of the Israelite army were sacrificing their lives for him, their beloved king. The king is apparently unconcerned as he rises in the evening time and takes a casual stroll on the rooftop. This is the beginning of David's downfall. We soon start to see how the story unfolds in the enemy's favour. Let's pause here for a second.

As we highlighted earlier, for sin to take place there must be temptation. From inception, for Eve to pick the fruit, she had to be tempted. Sin is choosing to give into that temptation while virtue occurs when we choose to be obedient to the will of God. The major learning from the first two verses of Samuel 11 are that sometimes we create ripe opportunities for temptation due to our abdication of responsibility. At the heart of this abandonment of responsibility is actually the sin of sloth. Unlike most sins which are usually grave acts which are committed, sloth is actually a sin of omission. It is the deliberate avoidance of spiritual or physical work. The only problem with this *omitting* of responsibility is that it is usually the starting point of *committing* some grave act. We may ask ourselves, 'well what is the problem with casually lying around doing nothing?' The problem is our minds are never "doing nothing"; even when we are not consciously engaged, we are subconsciously engaged in some way.

Proverbs 16:27 tells us "Idle hands are the devil's workshop, idle lips are his mouthpiece". For example, in my interaction with several young people who have struggled with pornography addiction, many of them have admitted that many of the times they wound up viewing pornography were the times when they were home alone with nothing else to do. This does not necessarily mean that they had nothing better to do, it simply means they *chose* not to engage themselves more productively. I am always aghast when people express feelings of boredom when there are infinite ways in which we can engage ourselves virtuously. More often than not, however, the fact seems to be that it is not that there was nothing better to be done, rather, it was that we chose to abdicate responsibility of the moment for something more appealing. Let's face it, disregarding infants, we all have something for which we are immediately responsible, which should be our primary concern, however, we may not always 'feel compelled' to do that. That's fine. The danger in that, though, is that we must be prepared to fight the competing elements to do both right and wrong that will come. Sadly though, most times the wrong choice is the choice which will grant immediate satisfaction at the expense of long term consequence. So in the quest for the shot of dopamine we receive, we forsake virtue for a few moments of bliss.

We ought to recognize that it starts in the mind. It starts with the decision to not do what you should do. The point where it is decided "I am not going to do what I should do at this moment, I do not have a better alternative, but I just don't want to." When we read above, we realize that this was David's decision and that lust, adultery and murder were the consequence of the small decision to not do what he should have been doing. Combine that with the eternal battle that is on for our souls by an evil one and we have ourselves quite an impending disaster.

In chaos theory, the **butterfly effect** is the sensitive dependence on initial conditions in which a small change in one state of a deterministic nonlinear system can result in large differences in a later state. Quite simply, change one minor event in our lives and it drastically changes the outcome of future events. Let's take David's example above. Let's suppose David decided to take up his responsibility and go to war with Joab and his army. He would not have been on his rooftop strolling. He would not have seen Bathsheba. He would not have committed adultery. He would not have murdered Uriah. However good or bad the eventual outcome of his decision, many of the tragedies it caused could have been avoided by a small change in the initial conditions. Of course this example is hypothetical as we cannot accurately predict what David's consequent decisions would have been even if he adopted his responsibility but we do know that there would not have been an opportunity to see Bathsheba from the rooftop in that moment, we can infer the rest. It should also illustrate the unknown future consequences of not just our small decisions but also our non-decisions. I would like to emphasize that our decision not to act can be just as bad or worse than making a bad decision.

In verse 3 he sees Bathsheba bathing and is attracted to her and asks about her. He is told that she is the daughter of Eliam and the wife of Uriah the Hittite. To a man of integrity or character, the fact that Bathsheba was married and in fact married to one of his leading men in battle, should have been a deterrent to end further pursuits. In this moment, David like many of us was faced with a decision to either pursue his carnal vices or do what he knew to be right. David like many of us chose the former over the latter and the scene continues. Verse 4 tells us he sent for her and slept with her. We are not told if she was willing or not, however, it would be reasonable to assume that since she was married there would have been some sort of reluctance to proceed with the act. The second deterrent present was that she was menstruating as verse 5 mentioned her unclean nature. This still was not a deterrent for David as he continued his pursuit of vice until it was completed. A parallel must be made here. David knew the Jewish law well. He knew that adultery was in direct breach of the Ten Commandments and he also knew that women were considered unclean during the time of menstruation and that there should be abstinence. The point here is that knowing the Law is not enough, we must be empowered by God's spirit to keep it.

It almost sounds similar to Paul in Romans 7:21-23 above where he says the following "So I find this law at work: Although I want to do good, evil is right there with me. For in my inner being I delight in God's law; but I see another law at work in me, waging war against the law of my mind and making me a prisoner of the law of sin at work within me." If we didn't know that Paul wrote this letter to the Romans we could have almost assumed that it were the words of David. David clearly sounds like a man who has abandoned all virtue for the satisfaction of his immediate need. In these moments, he does not care that his armies are fighting a battle, he is unconcerned that Bathsheba is married and currently menstruating. All of these factors are of little significance in comparison to the desire for immediate satisfaction and pleasure. The examples of David and Paul should frighten us but let us extend it even further.

Peter walked with Jesus side by side for three years, grew with him and committed to serve him until the end but when accused of being one of his disciples, in the face of punishment, he denied even knowing him, three times. Judas who also shared in Jesus' ministry for three years was offered a reward, an immediate satisfaction just like David and he chose the satisfaction of thirty pieces of silver. David, Paul, Peter and Judas all teach us the point which Paul drives home - we know what's right, but in the face of temptation, we all choose ourselves over God at times. It should frighten us because it shows quite clearly that we all have a self-serving beast within that can be unlocked under the right conditions which is limitless in its quest if not restrained by the gift of self-control. Peter didn't plan to deny Christ, Judas didn't plan to betray him and David didn't plan to commit adultery. It all simply flowed out of small lapses in judgement, which is why we need to exercise great caution and wisdom with our decisions.

We will soon go into the implications of David's decisions but first reflect on your own life here for a moment, what decisions have you made that have sent your life into disarray? When did you find yourself in some sort of trouble because you neglected your responsibility and did something unbecoming? I remember preaching at a particular church and asking the congregation "How many of you all have done something you never thought you would have done and after asked yourselves, what got into me?" The nods were unanimous.

We all act out of character but if sin is the root and sin lives within us, are we acting out of character when we sin or when we do right? Are we sinful creatures that strive to do right or are we all good people that sometimes do wrong under specific circumstances? I must admit this question caused me trouble to find a conclusion especially when I found reasonable support on both sides for some time. I am more convinced of us being sinful, however, because I find that if left unchecked, human beings tend to negate responsibility. If you let a ball roll freely, it will not freely roll uphill. We are that ball and the hills are the responsibilities of our lives. We do not gravitate towards what is difficult. Living morally is difficult, satisfaction is easy and just like the ball, we will tend toward ease. To recognize this is to recognize that we need to be deliberate and intelligent in our quest for mastering the self. This is not a new concept but it has become an all but silent one in contemporary culture.

The books of Samuel were written 900 years before the birth of Christ. The book of Romans was written approximately 57-58 years after the birth of Christ. I was born almost 2000 years later and I find within myself the same pattern and if you are honest with yourselves, you will find the same also. We do what is right when it is easy to do what is right, but when is it ever easy to do right? If the people who lived and walked with Jesus everyday still found it incredibly easy to do what pleased them in a moment of temptation, then it points to a clear lack that exists within our design as human beings.

Is it even sensible then to write a book 2000 odd years later to encourage people to overcome sin and temptation? Is it wishful thinking? Precisely the opposite. I find that although there is the desire to do wrong etched within each one of us, we are blessed to have been given the gift of repentance and the supernatural gift of grace. The same man Paul who uttered words of despair in Romans 7 is the same individual who wrote "I have fought the good fight, I have finished the race, I have kept the faith" in the second letter of Timothy chapter 4. The same man David who commits shameful acts above is the same individual wrote the Psalms of the Bible. The grace of God saves, the grace of God transforms; the grace of God is that external agent that pushes the ball uphill. Although the capacity to do good is within us, it is not enough for us to earn salvation on our own. We must earnestly seek it out, cry out to God for it and let it permeate our lives from the inside out.

Verse 5 continues the treacherous tale: Bathsheba finds out she is pregnant and David's immediate plot to cover up begins. His first plan is to convince Uriah that the child is his own. So he calls Uriah from battle and sends him home to spend time with his wife. Uriah, however, being a man of integrity, finds it difficult to do such especially while his brothers were in battle and he sleeps outside the palace. David is annoyed at this and moves on to the second plan to cover up his immoral actions. Again it is clearly apparent how much David abandons his concern about everything and everyone except himself and his situation. As highlighted above, the self-serving beast is awakened. In verse 14 David commits yet another fatal error in judgement. He sends a note with Uriah, quite literally, Uriah's own death note. The note instructs Joab to place Uriah in the heat of the battle and have the troops pull back so he is struck down. David's plan is successful and Uriah is killed and David's third major sin is committed. What started off as rejecting responsibility quickly developed into lust, adultery and now murder. While the sins are grave, the genesis of it all should be the focus since this is where we have control. The difficulty to redeem a sinful situation increases exponentially when we have opened the doors of our sinful appetite. Like David, sometimes these doors can only be closed after much damage is done.

The end of the discourse sums up the entire narrative quite succinctly: "But the thing David had done displeased the Lord." David tried as best as he could to take matters into his own hands and right his wrongs through his own means, firstly by trying to have Uriah sleep with his wife to claim the child that she would bear, secondly by having him killed when the first plan didn't work and thirdly by making Bathsheba his wife. All of these were attempts to remedy the situation which he created but one thing is certain in the story of David - because God is just, he always rewards obedience and by that same standard he always brings disobedience to justice.

It should emphasize in our own lives the freedom and peace that comes through obedience. God does not want to teach us difficult lessons. He does not want us to stumble and fall and have to redeem situations which we have thoroughly messed up but he does it out of love for us. What may seem like incredibly sordid and embarrassing situations, God can still redeem, even though his will is always that we avoid sin rather than to redeem us from the consequences of it. At this point we can ask the question "How can we know that since we are not God?" I would respond by saying that we know enough about God from his word to know that he has a divine plan for each one of us which he would like us to obey but not one which he will force us to obey. Grace helps us obey and when we fail mercy helps us to be redeemed but it is not the intention that we fail in order that we may be redeemed. Let's think of a practical example, most organizations have a first aid kit. It is there in the event that someone may injure themselves but it is not the intention that we will cut open our foreheads every day. God's mercy is our first aid kit. It is only there in the event that we need it. It is not there to be abused or used if it is not needed. Neither is it there to be used in the anticipation of an injury. Our aim is not to fall, our aim is to walk and walk well but like children we will stumble, creep, fall then walk until we do it well. Our parents do not complain when we stumble; rather, they pick us up and help us walk again. Similarly God helps us up but just like our parents, he intends that one day you will walk well! Do not lose hope.

The second part of the story of David involves a pivotal character called Nathan. He is illustrated below in 2 Samuel 12:

The LORD sent Nathan to David. When he came to him, he said, "There were two men in a certain town, one rich and the other poor. ² The rich man had a very large number of sheep and cattle, ³ but the poor man had nothing except one little ewe lamb he had bought. He raised it, and it grew up with him and his children. It shared his food, drank from his cup and even slept in his arms. It was like a daughter to him.

⁴ "Now a traveller came to the rich man, but the rich man refrained from taking one of his own sheep or cattle to prepare a meal for the traveller who had come to him. Instead, he took the ewe lamb that belonged to the poor man and prepared it for the one who had come to him."

⁵ David burned with anger against the man and said to Nathan, "As surely as the LORD lives, the man who did this must die! ⁶ He must pay for that lamb four times over, because he did such a thing and had no pity."

⁷ Then Nathan said to David, "You are the man! This is what the LORD, the God of Israel, says: 'I anointed you king over Israel, and I delivered you from the hand of Saul. ⁸ I gave your master's house to you, and your master's wives into your arms. I gave you all Israel and Judah. And if all this had been too little, I would have given you even more. ⁹ Why did you despise the word of the LORD by doing what is evil in his eyes? You struck down Uriah the Hittite with the sword and took his wife to be your own. You killed him with the sword of the Ammonites. ¹⁰ Now, therefore, the sword will never depart from your house, because you despised me and took the wife of Uriah the Hittite to be your own.'

¹¹ "This is what the LORD says: 'Out of your own household I am going to bring calamity on you. Before your very eyes I will take your wives and give them to one who is close to you, and he will sleep with your wives in broad daylight. ¹² You did it in secret, but I will do this thing in broad daylight before all Israel.'"

¹³ Then David said to Nathan, "I have sinned against the LORD."

Nathan replied, "The LORD has taken away your sin. You are not going to die. ¹⁴ But because by doing this you have shown utter contempt for the LORD, the son born to you will die."

¹⁵ After Nathan had gone home, the LORD struck the child that Uriah's wife had borne to David, and he became ill.

¹⁶ *David pleaded with God for the child. He fasted and spent the nights lying in sackcloth[b] on the ground.* ¹⁷ *The elders of his household stood beside him to get him up from the ground, but he refused, and he would not eat any food with them.*

¹⁸ *On the seventh day the child died. David's attendants were afraid to tell him that the child was dead, for they thought, "While the child was still living, he wouldn't listen to us when we spoke to him. How can we now tell him the child is dead? He may do something desperate."*

¹⁹ *David noticed that his attendants were whispering among themselves, and he realized the child was dead. "Is the child dead?" he asked.*

"Yes," they replied, "he is dead."

²⁰ *Then David got up from the ground. After he had washed, put on lotions and changed his clothes, he went into the house of the* LORD *and worshiped. Then he went to his own house, and at his request they served him food, and he ate.*

²¹ *His attendants asked him, "Why are you acting this way? While the child was alive, you fasted and wept, but now that the child is dead, you get up and eat!"*

²² *He answered, "While the child was still alive, I fasted and wept. I thought, 'Who knows? The* LORD *may be gracious to me and let the child live.'* ²³ *But now that he is dead, why should I go on fasting? Can I bring him back again? I will go to him, but he will not return to me."*

²⁴ Then David comforted his wife Bathsheba, and he went to her and made love to her. She gave birth to a son, and they named him Solomon. The LORD loved him; ²⁵ and because the LORD loved him, he sent word through Nathan the prophet to name him Jedidiah.

The introduction of the prophet Nathan is critical. God sends Nathan to David for the sole purpose of revealing his evil to him. He initially tells David a parable of injustice, in response to which David ironically feels much anger, failing to realise that the parable was actually about David himself. God often sends "Nathans" in our lives to open our eyes to the wrong that we are engaged in. Quite similarly, like David, we may initially respond negatively out of our spiritual blindness or pride until we realize what the person has told us comes to pass. Many of us, like David, unfortunately never realize the mess we have made of our lives until someone specifically highlights it to us. Nathan highlights two clear points to David, firstly, he opens David's eyes to the wrong he has done. Secondly, he highlights God's justice. It is not until David sees that the wrath of God will soon be upon him that he decides to repent in verse 13 and sadly this is how it is for many of us as well.

Heaven *should* be enough for us to do right but it is not so sometimes; hellish circumstances need to shock us into reality and those circumstances are a direct result of God's justice. This often manifests itself in our lives in many different ways. We often bear many temporal consequences to our actions in our lives for us to realize our errant ways.

Sometimes we often end up in dire circumstances before we come to our senses and realize that there is a better life.

This is the inherent theme in the story of the prodigal son. The son had his father's inheritance awaiting him, however, he decided that he wanted it immediately and wanted to experience the thrills of life. After living a life of debauchery, the utility (as we described previously) faded leaving him empty and dejected. Soon he realized that his most sensible choice was to return home. It was not the father's wish that the son leave for a life of debauchery. He did not want him to but it was the son's sinful lifestyle that brought him to the realization of the life he abandoned. It was when the son's money ran out and he was forced to feed pigs did he realize that he needed to swallow his pride, repent of his sinful ways and return to his father! Very similar to the prodigal son, it is not until David starts enduring God's justice that he comes to his need for repentance and voices in verse 13 "I have sinned against the Lord".

The other salient point to be realized in this part of the story is that although David was repentant and mercy was shown to him, he still faced the Lord's justice while on earth, that being the death of the child which Bathsheba bore. David prayed and fasted but God's justice was set. It should emphasize clearly to us the nature of God. As said previously, God's nature is love but it is also justice. Just as our obedience is rewarded, so to we must learn difficult lessons through the times we are disobedient. The prodigal son endured his hardship because of his disobedience, David did also. David would endure much suffering including having his own son have intercourse with one of his concubines. The old adage of 'what goes around, comes around' rings true here, some also refer to this concept as 'karma'. In the Christian context, we refer to it as reaping the just fruits of our actions whether good or bad. We reap what we sow both in this life and the next, and that should be something worth considering seriously.

The story of David is incomplete however, if we do not talk about his redemption. David was a man after God's heart and when we read Psalm 51, we read not of a man who failed God proudly but a man crying out to God from the depths of his heart. Psalm 51 has widely been modelled as a token psalm of repentance because it emulates clearly the recognition of one's shortcomings and the deep yearning for God's mercy and transformation upon us. It should be a psalm we read daily. Reflecting upon it should allow us to realize that even though David made incredibly poor decisions that led to tremendous suffering, through his pure and genuine repentance, he was able to find God's heart once again. Let us take a look at a few of the verses below:

<u>Psalm 51: 1-4</u>
"Have mercy on me, O God, in your faithful love,
in your great tenderness wipe away my offences;
wash me clean from my guilt, purify me from my sin.
For I am well aware of my offences, my sin is constantly in mind.
Against you, you alone, I have sinned, I have done what you see to be wrong,
that you may show your saving justice when you pass sentence,
and your victory may appear when you give judgement"

To live victoriously, we must be repentant like David. There will be moments when we abdicate our responsibility, moments where we choose to do what pleases ourselves and moments when God will send people into our lives to highlight where we have fallen short. In these moments we can either choose to be stubborn and prideful or repentant and humble. Let us choose David's response. Let us resolve to be humble like David above and cry out to God when we have sinned regardless of how embarrassing, shameful or hurtful or actions may have been.

Although God can redeem us regardless of how far off course we have gone, we do not know how much more impactful and powerful David could have been had he been more obedient to God but we do have a glimpse into how much suffering could have been avoided. There are many things we can learn from the story of David in terms of making better decisions but ultimately, we should understand that our first call is not to be restored by God but to be obedient so that restoration is not necessary.

Reflection on Victory

- Do I recognize that I am in a daily spiritual battle?

- Am I taking the necessary steps required for spiritual victory?

- What are my daily spiritual habits?

- Do I pray and read God's word enough?

- Are there responsibilities which I am consistently denying?

- Do I welcome the "Nathans" in my life that point out my wrongs?

Affirmations

- I am more than a conqueror!

- God has given me all I need to be victorious!

- I can do all things through Christ who strengthens me!

BEING A WITNESS

As said before, the life that God has given us is not merely for our own salvation but also to lead others to know the beauty of life that exists in Christ as well. Part of that is representing him well. I have highlighted a few points below that have helped me in my journey over the years. I pray it is a blessing for you.

1.   Get to know Jesus Christ.

This might sound cliché but it is not an oversimplification. Many Christians do not know Jesus. They know *of* Jesus and this is not enough. You will be challenged by many others with false versions of Jesus and you have to know him to be able to defend who he is and make him truly known. The truth is many of us have in our minds, a version of Jesus that we have inherited from someone, whether it's a televangelist, pastor, priest or the Internet. What's even more dangerous is that the version we know can be incredibly different from the actual person who lived, bled, died and rose 2000 years ago. So how do we get to know this person whose birth split time in two?

I would like to advocate for starters immersing yourselves fully in the gospels. Maybe starting with John and then working back through the other 3 synoptic (Matthew, Mark and Luke). While you read, observe the following:

1.   The authority with which Jesus spoke
2.   His wisdom in reference to the Old Testament
3.   His claims to divinity

4.   His fulfilments of the prophecies of the Old
        Testament. (Birth, Life, Death and Resurrection)

When you read the gospels and observe the references
above. Two things come to mind as CS Lewis puts it "Either
this man was, and is, the Son of God, or else a madman…"
His claims do not leave room for any other option. He was
not simply just a good man or a prophet. His claims
transcended those such as "The Father and I are one" John
10:30 and "Before Abraham ever was, I am" John 8:58.
Claiming to be one with God the Father and claiming to
exist before someone who lived about 2000 years before him
are certainly not the words of any ordinary man.

Our conclusions about Jesus then must either be fully taking
him at his words or not. When we consider the convergence
of the biblical and secular authors about who this individual
is, there is little to no evidence to suggest that he was not
who he said he was and an overwhelming base of
archaeological and historical evidence suggesting that he
was.

While scholars such as Richard Dawkins may choose to be
skeptical, *in spite of* the overwhelming evidence, no credible
scholar disputes the fact that the evidence is there. Non-
belief does not erase that.

I will not go off on a tangent here about defending Jesus'
divinity rather, I recommend "The Case for Christ" by Lee
Strobel for that. The emphasis here will remain on
encouraging you to immerse yourself fully in the four
gospels through prayer and come to your own conclusions.

It is how I started to understand fully who the person of Jesus is and why representing him well is not just something we should think about doing well but something that is absolutely necessary for anyone who decides to take up the daily challenge of denying ourselves, taking up our crosses and following him.

2.   Put Him at the centre of your life.

After coming to know him, we come to understand why it is absolutely necessary to place him at the centre of our lives!

To quote one of my favourite priests from the USA Fr. Mike Schmidt, "Do you want to follow Jesus or do you just want to be known for following Jesus?" In the wave of today's social media identity-driven world, I believe the question is absolutely necessary for us to ask ourselves. Most young people (younger millennials and Generation Z particularly) seem to thrive for a following or platform as a means of validation and significance. However, to chase this will always be elusive. In fact, to seek ultimate validation anywhere outside of Christ will always be elusive because you will be building your house on shifting sand.

Christ is the foundation on which our church is built and thus, he must be the rock on which our faith is built, it is he who validates us. In the midst of the ever-changing tide of liberalism, secularism, post-modernism, atheism, nihilism and all the other worldviews that try to force Christians into perpetual silence, it is only by keeping our eyes solely fixed on Jesus and his voice are we able to burn with passion not just simply to share the life that we live in Christ but to share who HE is! To convert people to Christ, they must be able to see him present in us and that can only come if our focus is on him.

We spoke earlier about sheep listening to the voice of their shepherd, when we immerse ourselves consistently in his word, we become familiar with the way in which Jesus speaks, the tone, the texture of his language, what he expects from us in a particular situation. It is then we are able to differentiate his voice in our lives from others because his voice remains consistent with his written word.

When we live under the guidance of his voice, people no longer see us, but they see Christ in us and this is the goal! People don't respond to us, they respond to Christ moving in us.

3.   Your public witness is a reflection of your private prayer life

The first two points addressed knowing him and ensuring that he is the foundation of our lives.

The third point deals with building our relationship with him. We can only have a serious relationship with him if our lifestyle is one of prayer. People, especially young people, tend to be turned off by a message of prayer because the perception can be that prayer is boring or even a waste of time in today's fast paced society. However, if we understand that it is through prayer that our victories are won, we would live differently.

Prayer is not always what we perceive it to be. Sure, we can kneel at our bedsides or at church and cry out to God and that is an excellent way of connecting our hearts to him but too often we limit prayer to a particular style, overlooking the fact that it is simply communication with God. Communication and love are the foundation of any healthy relationship and therefore we will only grow in love with God if we spend time talking to him and also actively listening to his voice in our lives.

To share the fruits of Christ and his Holy Spirit with another, we must have that fruit and his Spirit dwelling within us and that can only come from a deep personal connection to Christ. We cannot pour from an empty cup. We must bear in mind that Christianity points to Jesus, his love for us and our love for him. We will only be compelled to share about him if we have a relationship with him.

Any relationship we strive to build takes work. It takes time, patience, effort but most importantly it takes love. The upside is God is always infinitely more interested in us than we are in him so he will always continue drawing us to him. We just need to be open and willing.

Our public witness therefore is completely dependent on the depth of our willingness to respond to his promptings in our life. Once we do, we find that we move from trying to spend time with him to *wanting* to spend time with him.

The simple equation as far as I can tell is this:
Souls are inherently attracted to Christ (whether they know it or not).

Therefore souls are attracted to souls that are attracted to Christ.

To be an effective witness, people must be able to tangibly recognize your relationship with Christ through the fruit of your life.

## 4.	Be genuine about your journey.

People are often converted when they truly encounter a sense of genuineness about someone's belief in Christ. The converse, however, is also true and I would say even more magnified! People are incredibly turned off and sometimes leave church permanently by encountering those who seem to be disingenuous about their belief in Christ. People can easily sense when someone does not genuinely believe the words that they speak and we must always bear this in mind. We should never speak anything that we do not truly believe because the effect would be discouraging.

I have seen many fall prey to this, even myself in my earlier years of this journey. I tried to be somewhere I was not yet and God taught me a serious lesson in humility. It is far more impactful to speak of being at a particular place in your journey only when you have arrived at that place and that may require patience. It is easy to want another's faith, fervour or zeal, but we do not know the journey God had to take another through to bring them to that place. Embrace your journey. Embrace where you are right now and share from that genuine place. There is someone, somewhere, waiting to hear exactly who you are and what you have been through who will be inspired by this precise moment of your life. Don't rob them of that by rushing your journey trying to be someone you are not.

5.   Obedience is the fruit of love.

The truth is Christianity is not a handbook where we share the rules we abide by, and this is not the manner in which it should be viewed. Christianity, rather, is centred on an encounter with a person and is hinged on a relationship with that person. Aside from those with a mental condition, we generally do not enjoy hurting the people we love. If a husband truly loves his wife in the agape way mentioned in an earlier chapter, then he would truly enjoy seeing her happy and would actively want to avoid the things that would make her upset. In fact it would greatly hurt him to see her hurt from his actions. In a much more infinite but similar sense, this is how we should think of our relationship with Jesus. Our thinking should shift from "I should obey because it's the right thing to do" to rather "Because I know the life that he has promised me out of love, I will live my life pleasing to him out of love in return". Many Christians who view Christianity as a set of rules often have an incredibly difficult time overcoming sin because the approach is misaligned. The source of our victory is the power of the Holy Spirit. Once we are reliant on this, we come into the agape love and power that we need to be victorious.

Others also easily sense actions that are done out of routine as opposed to those out of love. If the apostles served Christ out of routine, it would have been very easy for them to renounce their faith the moment severe persecution came their way. However, love was the driving factor that pushed them to persevere to the end and it was the catalyst for the spread of the faith to the ends of the earth. People are not converted out of routine, they are converted out of love. I have probably encountered thousands of persons on my journey thus far and I could probably count on one hand those who left an indelible impact on my heart, some of whom were even younger than I am. I remember an encounter with one particular girl who was just about sixteen years old, who I love like a sister. I was truly drained one day after ministry and she simply told me "God sees your heart Jameke, he knows how you feel and he is with you." It was exactly what I needed to hear at that moment and it lifted my entire spirit not because it was incredibly eloquent but because of the love and the genuine place from which it came.

This is essentially what it's all about - God is love, and it is love that transforms hearts, minds and souls. If love is the focus, obedience will be the fruit of that. The message here is that it does not matter who you are or where you are from, if you are open to God's love, he will use you to impact others as he sees fit. He will not force that openness however, but he does expect that once you experience his love, you will choose it. In fact, I would argue that once you do experience his love it is incredibly difficult to want to choose anything else.

Peter's example in the gospel of John indicates this. Immediately after Jesus gives his teaching on eating his flesh and drinking his blood, many of his disciples left him. He then turned to Peter and asks "Will you also leave?"

Peter responds "Lord, to whom shall we go, you have the message of eternal life"

Peter understood that even though this was a difficult teaching to stomach, something within him recognized that within the person of Jesus, there was something divine that resonated deeply within him. More precisely, Peter recognized truth and love. We are innately drawn to truth and love.

6.   Allow yourself to be used even in your weak moments.

This was a difficult one for me to learn. Who wants to encourage someone when they themselves need encouragement? If we're honest, no one particularly. It is something that is contradictory to our nature. We naturally want to do the things that are comfortable or easy but as we should realize by now, God does not call us to comfort, he often calls us to rise above our feelings to be used for his glory. I recount one particular moment when I had to preach at a particular prayer meeting and had the absolute worst day: filled with discouragement, disagreements on work, frustration while driving home and issues in my relationship at the time. I remember thinking to myself that it was literally the worst possible day for me to stand and face a congregation and tell them anything good about the Lord or about trusting in him, because in those moments I did not even want to hear anything encouraging myself.

I could have easily made up an excuse to get out of the preaching, but something made me swallow the negativity, say a small prayer and prepare a short preaching moments before the prayer meeting started. I remember walking up to the microphone and facing the congregation, thinking to myself, "Lord, you have to do this because right now I just don't have it in me". It turns out sometimes, that is all we need to let God know. He just wants our "Yes". He always knows how we feel but he still wants to see if we will trust him in those moments. It turns out that preaching that night was one of the most powerful experiences. I remember so many people came up to me after thanking me for encouraging them and saying exactly what they needed to hear. I recall being in awe because I almost robbed a congregation of people from being encouraged and being spiritually fed because of the "frustrations" of my day. It truly blew me away that God used me in my most unprepared, unwilling moments to encourage others and it truly opened my eyes, making me realize that this journey is so much more about him than it is about me. With my "Yes", God can move mountains, so why limit an infinitely powerful God because of a "hard" day. That day not only encouraged the congregation but it truly encouraged me as well to see what God had done through me. He lit a spark and changed my outlook that day because of my "Yes" and he will do the same for you.

Christianity will take you through the ringer of emotions. You will never always feel to serve Jesus. You will never always feel to sing or praise or pray. There are times when it will be tremendously difficult and as highlighted in the first chapter on suffering, you may even endure true hardships like the apostles for attempting to serve God. However, commitment through the hardships provides grace and that grace leads to peace, peace within the storms and triumphs through the tragedies, but to be a witness one thing remains abundantly clear you must be courageous enough to say "YES".

7.   Go where the spirit leads you

You are not called to save everyone. You are called to save those who God's Spirit leads you to save. Let me expand on this a bit. The words of Jesus are that we are called to preach his gospel to the ends of the earth but it does not necessarily mean that each of us are called to be international missionaries spreading the words of Christ to the ends of the earth; the spirit will move in each of us differently to fulfil God's will. It does mean, however, that we are called to be very attentive to the voice of the Holy Spirit in our life to know when to speak, to whom to speak, what to say and when to remain silent. The spirit will use many of us in different places and in different ways. You may be called to travel the word preaching the gospel while others may be called to be a witness in their very families.

Often times we can find ourselves trying to win arguments against others with regards to religion and faith, not because God has led us to the conversion of a soul but because of our own proclivity to win an argument. We must keep the perspective. Our call is to save souls, not win arguments. If by winning an argument a soul is saved then the means has justified the end since it would have been the Spirit of God which brought the person to an understanding and acceptance. However, if the end in our minds is winning an argument, we have missed the point of it all. Winning an argument means nothing if it does not lead another to repentance and understanding of who Jesus is and what he did for us.

We also need to consider two important points when witnessing to others. We may be trying repeatedly to bring another to an understanding of who Jesus is but they may just not be ready. This is why we need to rely on the Holy Spirit to guide us to those with open hearts. If not, we will simply be wasting energy, effort and time. People come to an understanding of different things at different times in their lives and we need to be tolerant with others on their journeys, still standing for truth but understanding also that we were not always where we are now and that we are called to appreciate another's process just as others were patient with our own. My grandmother prayed for me for years. She took me to church from as early as I could remember but eventually I had to come to a personal decision of my own to pursue a relationship with Christ; that took nineteen years. It was not something that she could force on me; remember the relationship God calls us into is a relationship of love and if it is forced, it isn't love.

Saul had to go through his own journey before Jesus physically appeared to him and brought him to conversion; similarly, David had to make a terrible mess of his life before he came to repentance. As said before, Christianity is about our personal relationship with Jesus and each relationship is formed by their own unique encounter and the time that is spent building it. When we understand that, we become significantly more patient with others.

The second point is that God may have someone else in mind other than you, who may be more effective at bringing an understanding of who he is to a particular person. The point here is simply that there are people who will not be convicted by your life's stories or anything you say but will be convicted by someone else and that's fine. This does not mean that either of us are better than each other spiritually, it simply means that people resonate differently to different people because of the different experiences we all face. Someone who lost a parent in a gruesome manner may be able to resonate with my testimony shared earlier but it may fall on deaf ears to a mother who may have had an abortion and is looking for another who may understand.

We are all different vessels: different vessels with different stories, skills, gifts and testimonies. It is the same spirit at work but used in a variety of ways. I may be able to preach to a large crowd and bring conversion, you may be able to have a deep one on one conversion and achieve the same, another may be able to pray for someone and achieve healing. It is the same spirit at work but recognizing that different people are used differently helps us understand in a deeper way how we are specifically called and who we are called to help. This helps us to be much more impactful with our words and our lives since we do not want to waste time with unnecessary conversations, arguments or frustrations.

As highlighted earlier in this book, though, we can only be attentive to the voice of God if we actively take the time to withdraw ourselves and listen.

Reflections on Being a Witness

- Can others easily see the light of Christ in me?

- Am I genuine with others about where I am on my journey?

- Do I put on a spiritual façade when doing spiritual things?

- How easily distracted am I when I spend time in prayer?

- Can I share about God in my weakest moments?

- Do I find myself trying to win arguments more than souls?

Affirmations

- My weakness is a continuous reminder that I am dependent on God.

- I will identify one habit that I will spend less time on and replace with personal prayer.

- I will be genuine and honest with God about where I am in my journey.

- I will be genuine and honest with others about where I am in my journey.

- I will evaluate myself daily to determine if my actions are consistent with my words.

PURPOSE

I have developed a particular habit as I enter and leave my current job every day, I look up at the sky. It centers me and reminds me that there is something more. It reminds me of my miniscule presence in this vast universe and that while miniscule, God handcrafted a purpose and plan for my life that is specific to me and no one else.

The first step in discovering my purpose was recognizing that I was uniquely made. I have been given talents, abilities, quirks, idiosyncrasies, flaws and most importantly experiences which have all shaped me into the person I am today. In all that I have proposed earlier, I have stated that this journey is not meant to be lived in an insular manner. God did not design us to exist in a vacuum, in fact, it is quite the opposite. Every experience and trial that you have faced and will face can be used to build and strengthen the character of another as well as your own and in a very material way, lead someone to the source of truth in God through Christ. When I realized how powerfully the experiences that I have been through have touched and impacted the lives of others, I understood quite clearly that in my pain eleven years ago, God knew the long term plan. He knew the healing that my story would bring to people, he knew the breakthroughs that would come as well as the peace and joy that he would fill within my heart and the strengthened spirit he would give me. But I am no different from you.

Your purpose lies within your story, the sum total of your experiences. The only way you can discover your own reason for being here is by first embracing who God called you to be which is his child. This requires recognizing that within that call you may be messed up, addicted, broken, angry, depressed, jealous, hurt, bitter, and a few other unpleasant states along the way. Be patient. The bigger picture is yet to be revealed and when it is, things will make sense. Things become complete. Let the story unfold. It is the most overwhelmingly joyous experience to sit back and watch God change lives through your broken experiences. The irony is that many times you must first be completely broken before you are made completely whole. Within the mess though, just like David, your broken story can add value and hope to this world.

In today's society transformation requires withdrawal, withdrawal from the busyness of life and its many distractions, even sometimes working for the Lord. Sometimes we become so engulfed in our routine that we forget the purpose of it all or overlook many ways in which we can enhance ourselves. Self-reflection is absolutely necessary for elevation and growth. God does not speak in noise. He speaks in silence. He does not reveal in noise, he reveals in silence. Many times the answers and enlightenment that we seek seem to not be forthcoming because we do not place ourselves in the right environment to hear such answers. Just as seeds need good soil to grow, the human heart needs silence to grow and hear the voice of the Father.

We are all playing a part in his story - every human being - and he is opening and closing doors to lead and guide allowing all of our paths to interconnect for each other's upliftment and ultimately salvation. Sadly, not all will choose his path regardless of the interventions made, a necessary consequence of creating beings out of love. Love requires freedom and unfortunately for some, freedom allows the opportunity for bad choices. This must not discourage us from the journey. Although all were meant to be saved, all will not be, but it does not mean that we must abandon our responsibility of trying. We must appreciate the fact that we have been given the opportunity and privilege to give another the most priceless gift that we can ever give.

If we see someone dying of thirst and we have water, rationally speaking, most of us would share our water with the dying person. However, so many of us are dying spiritually without Christ and those of us who know better don't offer the life we know to be true. We must understand that Jesus' death was for all of humanity, not just a select few. He desires that we all take up our call to be lights within the darkness and water in the barren land. Faith grows as we find our own victories in this life through Christ; let us share those with others leading them to the source of ultimate victory. Jesus!

Reflections on Purpose

- Do I spend enough time in silence to hear God's voice in my life?

- Am I afraid of what God may be calling me to?

- Do I recognize that God's plan for my life will give my life the most meaning, purpose and fulfilment?

- What elements in my life currently prevent me from hearing the voice of God?

Affirmations

- I will live in the purpose that God has intended for my life!

- I will separate myself from daily distractions to actively listen to God's voice!

- I have a unique call placed on my life that God has given me that He has not given anyone else!

CONCLUSION

I am hopeful that this book has been a blessing for you. I pray that the points were written clearly and that messages resonated. I had no idea the project I would be undertaking when I first started writing this book in December 2017. I had no idea how challenging it would be. It allowed me to realize many things about myself while writing and it also made me realize how much effort and spiritual preparation it takes to allow yourself to be a transparent vessel to impart God's wisdom. My prayer while writing was simply that God would move through me to say what he wants me to say and less of my own articulation. I pray that I have done so well.

Many times I became discouraged, suffered writer's block and felt unworthy to write a book of this nature. I did not have a plan initially regarding the direction I wanted to go with it but as I started praying and writing, a framework developed and the subsequent structure emerged, which I know now was definitely the Holy Spirit. If this book has touched you in some way, praise God. If you only remember one line from it, praise God. If nothing resonated with you, praise God as well; it may not have been the right time. In all things, we give God praise for he alone has given the grace for this project and has been a recurrent theme within the book. It is infinitely more about him and less about me or you. My prayer is simply that we live victorious lives in Christ and if through the reading of this book, you have taken even the most miniscule step towards that goal, then I have fulfilled in some way the call that God has placed on my heart through this endeavor.

I want to encourage you no matter where you are on your journey, you can let that be your starting point. Regardless of what happened in the last year, month, hour or minute, new life in Christ begins the moment you make the decision to turn away from sin and head towards him. Your past only determines your end if you let it, however, you will have to choose Christ, consistently and often as long as you have life, if you wish to be continuously victorious. Know that sometimes you will lose, you will not feel worthy, you will give into temptation and you will fail and the guilt will be heavy. Resolve, however, that you will continue moving forward, you will continue to overcome, you will be who you are called to be. Resolve that regardless of how difficult the journey will become, you will keep your eyes focused on him and his eternal promises and most importantly commit to being driven, strengthened and guided by his Holy Spirit as it is he alone who will provide the eternal strength required to overcome the many trials of this life.

I chose not to be defined by the pits in my life but by the victories. You have the power to do the same through God's grace. Decide! Act! Conquer! Live the life worth living. Be blessed!

BIBLIOGRAPHY

- "Bill Gates Net Worth Is Bigger than GDP of 130 Countries." *Knoema*, 21 Feb. 2020, knoema.com/wqezguc/bill-gates-net-worth-is-bigger-than-gdp-of-130-countries

- Divorce Magazine. "US Divorce Statistics and Divorce Rates (2000 - 2017)." *Divorce Magazine*, 19 Aug. 2019, www.divorcemag.com/articles/us-divorce-statistics-and-divorce-rates-2000-2017.

- *Kolbe, The Saint from Auschwitz*, www.auschwitz.dk/kolbe.htm.

- Military.com. "Navy SEAL Training." *Military.com*, www.military.com/special-operations/training-to-be-a-navy-seal.html

- Samjshah, et al. "Math 55: The Hardest Freshman Course in the Country." *Continuous Everywhere but Differentiable Nowhere*, 12 Aug. 2012, samjshah.com/2008/06/06/math-55-the-hardest-freshman-course-in-the-country/

- "What Is Virtue and What Are the Four Cardinal Virtues?" *Catholic Straight Answers*, 21 May 2013, catholicstraightanswers.com/what-is-virtue-and-what-are-the-four-cardinal-virtues/

- Written by Joseph D'Urso, Breaking News Reporter. "How Much Would It Cost to End Hunger?" *World Economic Forum*, www.weforum.org/agenda/2015/07/how-much-would-it-cost-to-end-hunger/